# Knit-a-Bear

# Knit-a-Bear

## 15 huggable friends to make and dress for every occasion

### VAL PIERCE

The Taunton Press

**The Taunton Press**
Inspiration for hands-on living®

The Taunton Press, Inc., 63 South Main Street
PO Box 5506, Newtown, CT 06470-5506
email: tp@taunton.com

First published 2014 by
Guild of Master Craftsman Publications Ltd
Castle Place, 166 High Street, Lewes,
East Sussex BN7 1XU

**Publisher** Jonathan Bailey
**Production Manager** Jim Bulley
**Managing Editor** Gerrie Purcell
**Senior Project Editor** Dominique Page
**Editor** Jane Roe
**Pattern Checker** Jude Roust
**Americanizer** Judith Durant
**Managing Art Editor** Gilda Pacitti
**Designer** Ginny Zeal
**Photographer** Andrew Perris

Set in Geometric Slabserif and Doctor Soos
Color origination by GMC Reprographics
Printed and bound in China

# Contents

# Introduction

Knitting a toy for a special person, whether they're young or old, can bring lots of pleasure. An all-time favorite soft toy is the teddy bear. Most of us have had a treasured teddy at some point during our lives. Teddy bears appeal to all ages with their endearing expressions and soft, cuddly exteriors. They prove to be trusty playmates and friends, and children just love them.

For this book I have designed fifteen bears, all of which have their own special characteristics. There's a ballet bear that will delight children who love to dance, an adventurous camouflage bear that is ready for action, a bear ready for shopping with her purse, and even a mother bear with her cub. Some have complete outfits with accessories; others are wearing just a simple top or waistcoat. Most of the bears are similar in size, so it is possible to change the clothes around and dress them in a new outfit each day.

*Val*

# Before you start

# Yarns

The array of yarns available can be overwhelming. Going into a yarn store is like entering Aladdin's cave with marvelous colors, textures, and fibers everywhere you look. When choosing yarn to make toys it is wise to take into account the age of the person you will be knitting for. Babies and young children invariably put everything in their mouths, so using an eyelash yarn that may shed fibers isn't a good plan.

In this book, most of the yarns used are a good quality wool or wool blend, because they work up nicely and have good stitch definition. They also wash well if needed. Some of the bears have been created using speciality yarns that have a fluffy and furry appearance when knit up.
I have stated a yarn weight for these yarns so it is possible to substitute them; however, keep in mind that if you do substitute, your finished project will not be identical to the one shown in this book.

## Gauge swatches

Each project has a suggested gauge for the yarns used, and these are listed along with the materials section for each pattern. These are a guideline to help you when choosing your yarns. Gauge is important for most projects, but with toys a slight discrepancy won't cause too many problems. Obviously, if you substitute yarns your finished bear isn't going to look quite the same as the one in the book, but it will still be a very lovable and unique character. See page 28 for more information about checking gauge.

## Speciality yarns

Some of the bears in the book have been made using speciality yarns. These give a more realistic appearance to the finished bear since they resemble fur. When sewing with this yarn, use a large-eyed, blunt-ended needle and be careful when pulling the yarn through the work. It may not be possible for you to obtain the exact yarns I have used, but you will no doubt be able to substitute other similar yarns for them.

## Yarn weights

Terminology for yarn weights varies from country to country. Below is a handy guide to common terms. The US numbers refer to the standard weight system developed by the Craft Yarn Council of America (CYCA).

| US | UK | Australia /NZ |
|---|---|---|
| 0–Lace | 2 ply | 2 ply |
| 1–Sock or Fingering | 3 ply or 4 ply | 3 ply or 4 ply |
| 2–Sport | Some double knitting yarns | 5 ply |
| 3–DK/Light worsted | Double knitting | 8 ply |
| 4–Worsted | Aran | 10 ply |
| 5–Chunky | Bulky | 16 ply |
| 6–Bulky | Chunky | 20 ply |

# Tools

As with all good recipes, the ingredients go a very long way to the success of the finished product. Substitute the word "tools" for ingredients and the same principle applies to knitting. Having found a gorgeous pattern that you want to knit, it's no good starting your project without all the necessary basic equipment and knowledge needed to make it.

## Knitting needles

There are many types of knitting needle available, ranging from metal, plastic, and bamboo to beautiful rosewood needles. If you are just starting out, I suggest you choose some mid-range priced needles. Some come in sets, which is very useful since it is handy to have a variety of sizes. For the patterns in this book, you'll need sizes ranging from US 3 to 9 (3.25mm to 5.5mm/UK10 to 5).

## Needle size conversion chart

Different sizing systems are used around the world. In the US, needles are usually marked with both the US size and the metric equivalent.

| US | Metric | UK |
|---|---|---|
| 0 | 2mm | 14 |
| 1 | 2.25mm | 13 |
| 2 | 2.75mm | 12 |
| - | 3mm | 11 |
| 3 | 3.25mm | 10 |
| 4 | 3.5mm | - |
| 5 | 3.75mm | 9 |
| 6 | 4mm | 8 |
| 7 | 4.5mm | 7 |
| 8 | 5mm | 6 |
| 9 | 5.5mm | 5 |
| 10 | 6mm | 4 |
| 10.5 | 6.5mm | 3 |
| - | 7mm | 2 |
| 11 | 7.5mm | 1 |
| 13 | 8mm | 0 |
| 15 | 10mm | 000 |

## Other useful tools

A stitch holder is recommended to keep some live stitches safe while you continue to knit on others.

Stitch counters are invaluable if you need to remember how many rows you have worked and they are especially useful when working with some of the speciality yarns used in the book.

Stitch markers are used to mark a particular point in your work, such as a crucial bit of shaping. You can use purchased stitch markers or just tie a piece of yarn in a contrasting color to the work.

It is also a good idea to have a couple of crochet hooks on hand in case you drop a stitch and need to work it up through the fabric.

A tape measure is an absolute must for checking the size of your work, as is a set of blunt-ended sewing needles with large eyes for easy threading when assembling a garment or toy.

Last, but by no means least, it is a great idea to have a knitting bag to keep all your projects safely stored away while you are not working on them.

# Knitting techniques

Although most of the patterns in this book are straightforward, it is best if you have some knowledge of knitting before starting a project. In this chapter, you will find a basic guide to all the stitches used in this book. The instructions are given for right-handed knitters; if you are left-handed, you can either follow the right-handed instructions or reverse the hand-holding instructions.

### Slip knot

The first thing you need to do is make a slip knot, which forms the first stitch.

**Tip** Numerous tutorials for practically every technique used in knitting can be found on the Internet. These give extra information and visual instructions if you feel unsure of what you are doing.

1 Leave a tail of about 2"/5cm and hold it in your left hand; hold the ball end of the yarn in your right hand. Wind the yarn around the forefinger on your left hand. Slide the yarn off your finger and pull it through to form a loop. Transfer the loop to the needle.

2 Pull the yarn tail down to tighten it.

# Casting on

Once you have made the slip knot, you can begin to cast on. Casting on will form the first row of stitches on your needle and one edge of the finished project, usually the bottom or hem edge. There are many ways to cast on but the following two methods are the most widely used.

## The knitted-on method

1 Make a slip knot about 4"/10 cm from the yarn end on one needle and hold this needle in your left hand. Insert the right-hand needle through the front loop and under the left-hand needle. Now pass the working yarn (i.e. the yarn attached to the ball) under and over the tip of the right-hand needle.

2 With your right-hand needle, draw the yarn through the slip knot to form a stitch.

3 Transfer the new stitch to your left-hand needle, placing it next to the slip knot. Continue in this way until you have the required number of stitches.

## The long-tail or thumb method

1 Allow a sufficient length of yarn from the main ball for casting on the required number of stitches (you'll need roughly 1"/2.5 cm for each stitch). Make a slip knot on one needle and hold this in your right hand. Wind the tail-end of the yarn around the thumb of your left hand, from front to back, and hold firm.

2 Insert the tip of the needle through the thumb loop from front to back and wind the yarn in your left hand around the back of the tip of the needle and between the needle and your thumb.

3 Pull the new loop through the thumb loop, forming a stitch. Slip the stitch onto the needle close to the slip knot. Continue in this way until you have the required number of stitches.

# Knit stitch

Once you have mastered casting on you can begin to form the first of two fundamental movements in knitting. The knit stitch forms a flat vertical loop on the fabric face. When working back and forth with only the knit stitch, you create a simple furrowed fabric known as garter stitch.

1 Hold the needle with the cast-on stitches in your left hand. Keeping the yarn behind the work, hold the second needle in your right hand and insert it into the front of the first stitch. With your right forefinger, bring the yarn over and around the right-hand needle.

2 Pull the yarn through to create a new loop on the right needle.

3 Drop the stitch from the left needle. Continue for each stitch on the left-hand needle.

## Purl stitch

The purl stitch is the other key stitch that is used in knitting. When used for every other row along with the knit stitch it forms stockinette stitch, which is flat and smooth on one side and more raised and bumpy on the other. Once learned and mastered, these two stitches form the basis for a huge range of stitch patterns.

Working this method, the needle is put into the front of the stitch, then the yarn, which is held in the front, is wrapped over the back of the needle. Purl stitches tend to be a bit looser than knit ones so keep your fingers close to the work to help make the stitches more even.

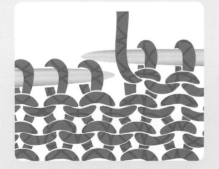

1 Hold the needle with the stitches in your left hand. Keep the yarn in front of the work.

2 Insert the point of the right-hand needle into the front of the first stitch on the left-hand needle. With your right forefinger, bring the yarn over the point of the right needle in a counterclockwise direction.

3 Bring the needle back through the stitch and pull through, creating a new stitch on the right-hand needle. Drop the stitch from the left needle. Continue for each stitch on the left-hand needle.

## Stitch patterns

### Garter stitch

Cast on any number of stitches.
Knit every row.

### Stockinette stitch

Cast on any number of stitches.
**Row 1 (right side):** Knit.
**Row 2 (wrong side):** Purl.

### Reverse stockinette stitch

Cast on any number of stitches.
**Row 1 (right side):** Purl.
**Row 2 (wrong side):** Knit.

### Seed stitch

Cast on an odd number of stitches.
**Row 1:** K1, *p1, k1; rep from * to
end of row.
Repeat row 1.
This can also be worked as double
seed stitch on a multiple of four
stitches.
**Rows 1 and 2:** * K2, *p2; rep from
* to end of row.
**Rows 3 and 4:** *P2, *k2; rep from
* to end of row.

### Rib stitch

**K1, P1 or 1 x 1 ribbing:** Single knit
stitches alternate with single purl
stitches, creating very narrow
columns. This stitch usually forms
the hems or neckbands on
garments and pulls in the work
tightly. To create K1, P1 ribbing,
cast on an even number of stitches.
**Row 1:** *K1, p1; rep from * to end
of row.
Repeat Row 1 for the length of
your piece.

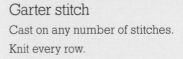

### Double rib stitch

**K2, P2 or 2 x 2 ribbing:** Two knit
stitches alternate with two purl
stitches. This stitch can also be
used for hems and neckbands but
it is more stretchy and pulls in less.
To create K2, P2 ribbing, cast on
a multiple of four stitches.
**Row 1:** *K2, p2; rep from * to end
of row
Repeat Row 1 for the length of
your piece.

## Binding off

This technique is used to provide a finished edge at the end of your work. It is also used for shaping and for making buttonholes. You normally bind off in knit stitch on the right side of the work, but patterns will tell you if you need to bind off on the wrong side or using a different stitch. When binding off, be careful not to pull the stitches too tightly or you will end up with a puckered edge that could make it difficult to assemble the pieces.

1 Knit the first two stitches. Keeping the yarn at the back of the work, insert the needle through the first stitch on the right hand needle. Lift the first stitch over the second stitch and off the needle.

2 Knit the next stitch so that you have two stitches on the right-hand needle again. Repeat the process until the desired number of stitches are bound off. You will have a single stitch left at the end of your binding off. Slip this stitch off the needle, cut the yarn, run the end of yarn through the stitch and pull tightly to secure.

## Practice

Once you have learned how to cast on, how to knit and purl, and how to bind off, it's a good idea to practice all of these techniques before moving on to the next section.

# Increasing

When you are knitting a project that requires shaping you will need to add stitches, which is called increasing. This technique is also necessary when you are creating certain stitch patterns, such as lace.

**Tip** It is very important that you follow the particular method of increasing stated in the pattern you are following. As a rule the make one (M1 or m1) method is always mentioned in abbreviations for that pattern.

## The bar method (kfb)

This frequently used method produces a small horizontal stitch on the right side of the work. You knit into the front and back of a stitch to make two stitches.

It creates a tiny "bump" on the right side of the work so the increase is visible in the fabric but is not noticeable when worked on the edge of a garment.

1 Knit a stitch in the usual way but do not remove it from the left-hand needle.

2 Insert the right-hand needle into the back of the same stitch and knit again. Move the stitches from the left-hand to the right-hand needle.

## Make one (M1 or m1)

With this method you pick up the horizontal strand between two stitches and knit or purl into it to form a new stitch.

Insert the left-hand needle from front to back under the horizontal strand between two stitches.

Knit or purl into the back of the strand with the right-hand needle.

Transfer the stitch onto the right-hand needle. The twist in the stitch prevents a gap from forming in the work.

# Decreasing

Sometimes when you are knitting you have to get rid of several stitches in a row, such as when you are shaping a piece of a toy or working an armhole or neckline in a garment. Binding off is the normal method used when more than three stitches need to be decreased. However, if only one or two stitches have to be decreased, either of the methods described below and on the next page can be used.

When working decreases on garments, they are normally done in pairs that are symmetrical, as on V-neck shaping or raglan sleeve shaping. Right slants are made by knitting or purling two stitches together through the front of both loops; left slants are made by working through the back of both loops. Slip stitch decreases slant in only one direction, from right to left in the knit stitch and from left to right in the purl stitch.

## Knitting two stitches together (k2tog)

### Right slant (k2tog)

1 Insert the tip of the right-hand needle in the next two stitches on the left-hand needle through the front of both loops. Bring the yarn around the needle and draw it through.

2 Transfer the new stitch to your right-hand needle.

### Left slant (k2tog tbl)

Insert the tip of the right hand needle in the next two stitches on the left-hand needle through the back of both loops. Bring the yarn around the needle.

Draw the thread through and transfer the new stitch to your right-hand needle.

## The slip-stitch decrease

This results in a slightly looser decrease than knitting two stitches together. When made on a knit row it slants from right to left and is abbreviated Sl1, k1, psso. A similar decrease can be made on a purl row, and it slants from left to right. It is abbreviated Sl1, p1, psso.

**On a knit row**

Slip one stitch from the left-hand needle onto the right-hand needle without knitting it, then knit the next stitch.

Insert the left-hand needle into the front of the slipped stitch on the right-hand needle and pull it over the knitted one, as you do when binding off (see page 19). The right-to-left slant made by this decrease in a knit row is used on the right side of the center of the work.

**On a purl row**

Slip one stitch from the left-hand needle onto the right-hand needle without purling it, then purl the next stitch.

Insert the left-hand needle into the front of the slipped stitch on the right-hand needle and pull it over the knitted one. The left-to-right slant made by this decrease in a purl row is used on the left side of the center of the work.

## Picking up stitches

When making toys or garments there are sometimes neckbands, collars, and possibly edgings where you will need to pick up stitches from the edge of the knitted fabric. These stitches need to be picked up evenly all around the edge for a neat, uniform finish.

## To pick up a stitch from an edge

| Hold the working yarn behind the completed piece and insert the knitting needle through it, between the rows and between the last two stitches of each row, from front to back.

2 Bring the yarn over the needle as if knitting and draw a loop of the yarn through to form a stitch. Continue until the correct number of stitches have been picked up.

# Changing colors

Using different colors to enhance your projects is another technique that will bring fun to your knitting. For some of the patterns in the book you will need to knit stripes or work a motif into the fabric, so this section will tell you how to join in new colors or work with more than one color in a row.

## Working from a chart

Color patterns are often charted on graph paper. Each square represents a stitch and each horizontal line of squares is a row of stitches. Some charts use different colors while others are black and white and have a key at the side with different symbols depicting different shades. Charts are read from bottom to top and from right to left for right-side rows and left to right for wrong-side rows. They are normally in stockinette stitch and odd-numbered rows will be knit and even-numbered rows will be purled.

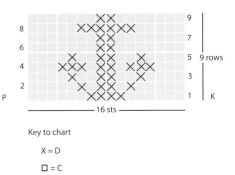

Key to chart

X = D

□ = C

The first stitch of a chart is the bottom one on the right. Placing a straight edge, such as a ruler or bookmark, under each row will help you keep your place in the chart when working the design.

## Adding new yarn at the start of a row

Use this method when working horizontal stripes.

Insert the right-hand needle into the first stitch on the left-hand needle and wrap the old and new yarns over the tip of the needle. Knit the stitch with both yarns.

Drop the old yarn and pick up the new yarn and continue to knit in the normal way.

## Adding a new yarn within the row

Follow this method when you will be using the original yarn again in the same row. The yarn not in use has to be carried along the back of the work; this is called stranding. This method is normally used over short distances, i.e. not more than four or five stitches. The weaving-in method is used when there are greater distances, i.e. more than six stitches, and is done by twisting the yarn to be carried along the back of the work and around the yarn you are working with at the time. It forms a much denser fabric.

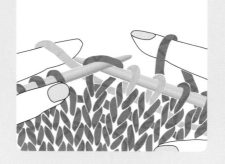

I Leaving the old yarn at the back of the work, insert the right-hand needle into the stitch. Wrap the new yarn over the needle and use it for the new stitch.

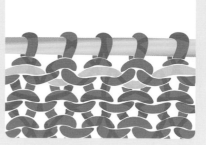

2 Continue knitting with the new yarn while carrying the old yarn across the back. On subsequent rows, purl the stitches in the usual manner.

## Intarsia

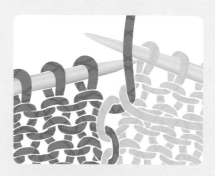

Intarsia is a technique used to incorporate areas of color into your knitting, such as motifs or shapes. For each block of contrasting color you use a different length of yarn. The yarn is not carried across the back of the work, but rather twisted around the main color at the edges of the secondary color. Wind the smaller amounts of yarns needed onto bobbins to keep the yarns from tangling while you knit.

## Duplicate stitch

This is a method of adding motifs to an already knitted garment and, if done correctly, it looks as though the motif is actually knitted into the fabric. You follow a chart as for the knitted version but instead of knitting the stitches, you work over each main-color knitted stitch with the contrast yarn threaded into a blunt-ended needle. Each "knit" stitch forms a V on the fabric and you embroider the contrast yarn over this V to build up the motif.

## Lace

Some of the patterns in this book use a lacy pattern, so you need to know how to create these stitches. These are abbreviated as yo (yarnover). A yarnover makes a new stitch and creates a "hole" in the fabric. You will then decrease a stitch in the same row to compensate and keep the stitch count the same.

To make a yarnover in stockinette stitch, bring the yarn over to the front of the work as if you were going to make a purl stitch. Loop the yarn over your right-hand needle and knit the next stitch.

The loop and new stitch are now on your right-hand needle. Knit to the end of the row.

On the following row and with the rest of the stitches, purl the loop in the usual way.

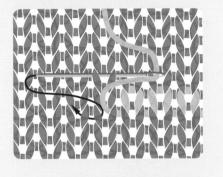

## Checking your gauge

When knitting toys you have to be careful with your gauge, but not to the same extent as you would with a garment. A slight variation in size will not matter a great deal in a toy, but if you are going to substitute yarns, be sure to check the gauge before starting on your project (see page 12 for the gauge swatch information about yarns used in this book).

To check the gauge, you need to make a gauge swatch. This is a 4-inch (10cm) square made using the stitch pattern, yarn, and needle size stated in the pattern.

Cast on the number of stitches and work the number of rows designated for 4 inches (10cm). When you have completed your swatch, pin it to a flat surface. Do not stretch it.

Measure the swatch horizontally and vertically. If your gauge does not match exactly that given in the pattern, change your needle size and knit another sample. One needle size will make a difference of about 1 stitch over 2 inches (5cm).

If your swatch is too small, your gauge is too tight and you should change to a larger needle. If your swatch is too large, your gauge is too loose and you should change to a smaller needle.

The type of yarn you use and the stitch pattern can also affect the gauge, so it's important to make a sample if you are changing either one from that in the instructions.

When checking gauge on a ribbed pattern, you need to pull the piece out to the correct width before measuring.

**Tip** Don't be afraid to change your needles. As long as the gauge works out correctly, your knitting is going to turn out the right size for that pattern.

# Correcting mistakes

While you are knitting it's always a good idea to check your work regularly for any errors; the sooner you pick up on them the quicker you'll be able to correct them.

Mark the row where the mistake occurred using a stitch marker at the end of the row. Carefully take your work off the needles and pull it back until you are one row above the error. To place the stitches back onto the needle, hold the yarn at the back of the work, insert the left needle into the front row of the first stitch below the unraveled row. Pull on the working yarn to remove the top stitch.

If you drop a stitch and it unravels down the fabric, use a crochet hook to retrieve the stitch and work it up row by row, picking up the strand of yarn behind the stitch on every row until you reach the top. Slip the stitch back onto the needle and continue working in the normal way.

# Assembly

Having spent many hours knitting all the pieces to make your toy, you now have to stitch all the pieces together and add the details. Don't be tempted to rush this step; clumsy seaming can ruin an otherwise beautifully knitted project.

## Sewing together

Toys need to be sewn together securely since they may have to withstand many hours of playtime and be pulled around by little hands. Go over areas more than once when sewing on arms, legs, and heads to ensure they won't pull off. Seams must also be sewn up securely—a backstitch seam works well for toys.

Very often toys' heads will appear to wobble when sewn in place and, seemingly, no matter how hard you try it is impossible to make them firm. This is a result of the head and body not being equally stuffed, i.e., if the head is too heavy then it will not sit correctly, and the same if the body is too solid and the head is under-stuffed. You can always add a little more stuffing to a piece by opening a tiny part of the seam, or you can remove stuffing in the same way.

To sew a head to a body, first tack it in place with a few stitches placed around the neck edge. This will hold it steady while you begin to sew the two pieces in place more

firmly. Join a stitch from the body to one from the head all the way around, pulling the yarn firmly. Check often that the head is straight, not too far back or too far forward. Mostly toys' heads will be facing front and straight. To get a really cute look on animals, angle the head slightly.

Some of the bears in the book have the head and body knitted in one piece. The head is then formed by running a thread all around a specifically marked row at the neck. The head part is stuffed first and then a needle threaded with matching yarn is woven in and out of each stitch on the marked row, beginning and ending at the center back. The yarn is then pulled tightly, forming the head. Make sure that the yarn is securely held when starting and finishing so it won't come undone and spoil the toy.

## Joining seams

There are various ways of joining seams on knitted fabrics. Garter stitch can be sewn up with the right sides of the pieces facing you. Catch the "tiny bumps" on the fabric together alternately from the pieces you are joining and pull them together firmly as you do. This will result in an almost invisible seam. You can join stockinette stitch the same way by picking up the horizontal strand between the V stitches on alternate pieces on the fabric to be joined and pulling it tightly—this is called mattress stitch.

## Stuffing and adding features

Stuffing toys and adding features are sometimes daunting tasks for the inexperienced. Refer to the picture of the toy you are making for help. Always use quality polyester stuffing and use small amounts at a time, teasing out the stuffing as you fill the piece of knitting. This will prevent large, lumpy bodies and heads and ensure a smooth and even feel to the toy. Don't over- or under-stuff your toy, and try to get arms and legs as even as possible, checking that they match in size and circumference as you work.

Wobbly heads can often be a huge problem when making toys this is often caused by either the head or body being over- or under-stuffed.

Clothes for a toy may not fit properly if the toy is over- or under-stuffed. I have provided dimensions for the waist measurements of the bears to help with this problem.

Adding the features is the final step. Look at the photograph of the toy you are making and place markers for the eyes and nose. Look at the size of the eyes you need to add. Practice stitches on a spare piece of fabric, and when you feel confident then work on your toy. If it doesn't look right, carefully unpick and try again. Patience is always rewarded where this is concerned.

Noses can be embroidered using straight stitches worked close together. Most of the noses in this

book are knitted, making it easier for you. When embroidering eyes, start with a French knot (see page 32) on one side, pull through to the other eye position and work a second French knot. Now continue to work extra stitches on each eye, pulling through alternately to each eye. This will also help to shape the nose. Don't pull in too tightly though, or you will distort the face.

As with anything, practice makes perfect so don't be disheartened if you are not satisfied with your first attempts. Just keep on trying and you will achieve the results you want.

## Twisted cord

Measure a length (or the number of lengths called for in the pattern) of yarn approximately four times longer than the desired length of finished cord. Fold the strand(s) in half and make a slipknot at the cut ends. Pass the slipknot over a doorknob or chair back spindle to anchor it and stand far enough away that the yarn comes straight out from the anchor, parallel to the floor.

Slip a crochet hook or pencil into the folded end and twist the yarn until it becomes taut.

Remove the end from the anchor, grasp the center of the twisted yarn and bring the ends together. Release the ends and the cord will twist on itself. Knot the ends.

## Tassel

Cut a piece of cardboard that is approximately twice the depth of your finished tassel. Wind the yarn around the card about fifteen or twenty times.

Thread matching yarn through the wraps at one end of the cardboard and tie around the top of the tassel tightly. Cut the yarn ends at the other end of the cardboard and remove.

Wrap a separate piece of yarn six times around the tassel about 1 inch from the tied end. Fasten off and push the yarn end inside the tassel to keep it neat. Trim the loose ends to make them even. Attach to a twisted cord if desired.

### SAFETY

Safety is paramount when finishing toys, especially if they are intended for very young children. Do not use buttons or beads on toys that will be given to babies or toddlers. You will see that I have not used buttons on any of the clothes for the teddy bears.

If you intend to use safety eyes, make sure they are properly fixed into the fabric. They consist of a plastic eye with a grooved shank, and a washer that pushes onto the back of the shank. You will hear the washer click into place when it's secured.

# Decorative embroidery

Simple embroidery stitches can add color and texture to a knitted garment.
I have used very simple embroidery stitches, such as chain stitch and lazy daisy
stitch, to create flowers and leaves. These are best worked with blunt-ended
needles so that you don't split the fabric when working through it.

### French knot

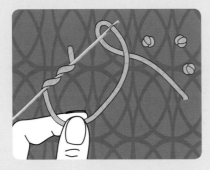

Bring the needle out of the knitted background from back to front; wrap the yarn around the needle two or three times. Use your thumb to hold it in place while pulling the needle through the wraps into the background a short distance from where it came out. The more times you wrap the yarn around the needle, the bigger the "knot."

### Chain stitch

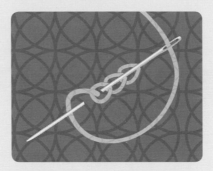

Start by bringing your needle up through the fabric as you would with any other stitch, then bring the needle back down through the same hole, slowly, in order to form a loop. Gently lay the loop flat against the fabric. Push the needle up on the inside of the tip of the loop, then back through the fabric again, this time securing the loop just made. The first chain is made. Continue in this manner to create consecutive loops.

### Lazy daisy stitch

This stitch is formed in the same way as a chain stitch but each "chain" radiates from the same central point to form a flower or leaf shape.

# Abbreviations & terminology

## Abbreviations

| | |
|---|---|
| **alt** | alternate |
| **beg** | beginning |
| **cm** | centimeter |
| **dec** | decrease |
| **foll** | following |
| **in.** | inch |
| **inc** | increase |
| **k** | knit |
| **kfb** | knit front and back |
| **ml** | make 1 |
| **p** | purl |
| **patt** | pattern |
| **psso** | pass slipped stitch over |
| **RS** | right side |
| **rem** | remaining |
| **rep** | repeat |
| **skpo** | sl1, k1, pass slipped stitch over |
| **st** | stitch |
| **St st** | stockinette stitch |
| **tbl** | through back loop |
| **tog** | together |
| **WS** | wrong side |
| **yo** | yarnover |

## US and UK terminology

| US | UK |
|---|---|
| Bind off | Cast off |
| Seed stitch | Moss stitch |
| Stockinette stitch | Stocking stitch |
| Yarnover | Yarn forward |

# The Projects

Henry

With his striped sweater, jolly neckerchief, and jaunty sailor's cap, Henry is sure to become a favorite companion for girls and boys alike. An anchor is knitted into the front of his sweater, but it can be duplicate-stitched onto the fabric if you prefer.

## YOU WILL NEED

### For Henry
Aran weight (CYCA #4) yarn:
100g (approximately 174 yds) in gray (A)
DK/Light worsted weight (CYCA #3) yarn:
50g (approximately 179 yds) in light gray (B)
Scraps of dark gray yarn for features

*Shown in:*
Rico Fashion Fur, 85% acrylic, 15% nylon
(87 yds/80m per 50g ball):
2 x 50g balls in 002 Gray
Sirdar Snuggly DK, 55% nylon, 45% acrylic
(179 yds/165m per 50g ball):
1 x 50g ball in 436 Light Gray

Needles size 9/5.5mm
Needles size 6/4mm
Quality polyester stuffing

### For the sailor outfit
DK/Light worsted weight (CYCA #3) yarn:
50g (approximately 179 yds) in white (C)
50g (approximately 179 yds) in red (D)
50g (approximately 179 yds) in navy blue (E)

*Shown in:*
Sirdar Snuggly DK:
1 x 50g ball white
1 x 50g ball red
1 x 50g ball navy

Needles size 6/4mm

**TiP** It isn't easy to count rows in this type of yarn so be sure to mark down the rows as you knit.

## KNITTING NOTES

### Gauge
12 sts and 16 rows to 4"/10cm for fur using size 9/5.5mm needles.
22 sts and 28 rows to 4"/10cm for DK yarn using size 6/4mm needles.

### Yarn notes
You may substitute the yarns listed for any eyelash or double knitting weight yarns, but check your gauge. If substituting the yarns your bear will not look quite the same as the one in the book.

### Measurements
11"/28cm tall when sitting. Circumference of belly when stuffed is about 13½"/34.5cm.

### Abbreviations
See page 33.

# Henry

## Head

Using size 9/5.5mm needles and A, cast on 10 sts.

**Next row:** Purl.

**Next row:** Inc in each stitch across row (20 sts).

Beg with a purl row, work 3 rows St st.

**Next row:** *K1, inc in next st; rep from * to end of row (30 sts).

Beg with a purl row, work 3 rows St st.

**Next row:** *K1, inc in next st; rep from * to end of row (45 sts).

Beg with a purl row, work 11 rows St st.

### Shape top of head

**Next row:** *K1, k2tog; rep from * to end of row (30 sts).

Beg with a purl row, work 3 rows St st.

**Next row:** K2tog across row (15 sts).

**Next row:** Purl.

Break yarn and run through sts left on needle. Draw up and fasten off.

## Body

Using size 9/5.5mm needles and A, cast on 10 sts.

**Next row:** Purl.

**Next row:** Inc in each stitch across row (20 sts).

Beg with a purl row, work 3 rows St st.

**Next row:** *K1, inc in next st; rep from * to end of row (30 sts).

Beg with a purl row, work 3 rows St st.

**Next row:** *K1, inc in next st; rep from * to end of row (45 sts).

Beg with a purl row, work 35 rows St st.

### Shape top of body

**Next row:** *K1, k2tog; rep from * to end of row (30 sts).

Beg with a purl row, work 3 rows St st.

**Next row:** K2tog across row (15 sts).

**Next row:** Purl.

Break yarn and run through sts left on needle. Draw up and fasten off.

## Muzzle

Using size 6/4mm needles and B,
cast on 8 sts.
**Next row:** Purl.
**Next row:** Inc in each st across
row (16 sts).
**Next row:** Purl.
**Next row:** *K1, inc in next st; rep
from * to last st, k1 (24 sts).
**Next row:** Purl.
Work 4 rows St st.
**Next row:** *K1, inc in next st; rep
from * to end of row (36 sts)
Work in St st for 6 rows and bind off.

## Legs
### make 2

Using size 9/5.5mm needles and A,
cast on 8 sts.
**Next row:** Purl.
**Next row:** Inc in each st across
row (16 sts).
Work in St st for 5 rows.
**Next row:** Inc 1 st at each end of
row (18 sts).
Work 3 rows St st.
**Next row:** *K2, inc in next st; rep
from * to end of row (24 sts).
Work 11 rows St st.
**Next row:** *K1, k2tog; rep from * to
end of row (16 sts).
Work 7 rows St st.
**Next row:** K5, inc in each of next
6 sts, k5 (22 sts).
**Next row:** Purl.
**Next row:** K5, (k1, inc 1) 6 times,
k5 (28 sts).
Work 5 rows St st and bind off
loosely.

## Arm pads
### make 2

Using size 6/4mm needles and B,
cast on 8 sts.
**Next row:** Purl.
**Next row:** K1, inc 1, knit to last
2 sts, inc1, k1 (10 sts).
**Next row:** Purl.
Rep last 2 rows to 14 sts.
Work in St st for 9 rows.
Bind off.

## Arms
### make 2

Using size 9/5.5mm needles and A,
cast on 8 sts.
**Next row:** Purl.
**Next row:** Inc in each st across
row (16 sts).
**Next row:** Purl.
Work 4 rows St st.
**Next row:** Inc 1 st at each end
(18 sts).
Work 13 rows St st.
**Next row:** *K2, inc in next st; rep
from * to end of row (24 sts).
Work 7 rows St st.
**Next row:** K2tog across row
(12 sts).
**Next row:** Purl.
**Next row:** K2tog across row (6 sts).
Bind off.

## Feet pads
## make 2

Using size 6/4mm needles and B,
cast on 8 sts.

**Next row:** Purl.

Inc 1 st at beg and end of next and
following alt (RS) rows until you
have 14 sts.

Work 11 rows in St st.

Dec 1 st at beg and end of next and
following alt (RS) rows until you
have 8 sts. Bind off.

## Ears
## make 2

Using size 9/5.5mm needles and A,
cast on 8 sts.

**Next row:** Purl.

**Next row:** Inc in each st across
row (16 sts).

Work 5 rows St st.

**Next row:** K2tog across row (8 sts).

**Next row:** Purl.

**Next row:** K2tog across row (4 sts).
Bind off.

## Assembly

Sewing up with this type of yarn is challenging. Use a big-eyed, blunt-ended needle and short lengths of yarn. Seams will run down the back of the head and body, and the undersides of the arms and legs.

Sew the body seam first, leaving the cast-on end open for stuffing. Stuff firmly to a nice rounded shape and close the gap. Sew the head the same way, leaving an opening to stuff. Stuff firmly. Sew the seams on the arms, leaving an edge open for stuffing. To stuff the arms, push plenty of stuffing down into the paw first, and then continue stuffing the rest of the arm. Pin the arm pads in position on each lower paw. Sew neatly in place.

Sew the seams on the legs, leaving the base open for sewing on the foot pads. Stuff the legs, then pin each foot pad in place around the foot opening, adding more stuffing if needed. Carefully sew the foot pad in place around the opening. With dark gray yarn, embroider claws on the paws and feet with long stitches.

Sew the muzzle seam; this will run underneath. Pin the muzzle to the front of the bear's head and add stuffing to shape. It may take a bit of time and patience to get this to look right. When you're satisfied, sew the muzzle onto the face, adding more stuffing as necessary. Embroider a nose, mouth, and eyes with dark gray yarn. Pin the ears onto each side of the head, making sure they are level. Curl the ears into a semicircular shape, then stitch in place onto the head with matching yarn.

Assemble the bear in a sitting position. Pin the legs in place first, making them level, and sew in place. Next pin the arms in position and sew firmly in place. Finally, sew the bear's head onto the body.

# Sailor outfit

## Sweater back

Using size 6/4mm needles and E, cast on 42 sts.

Work 6 rows in k2, p2 rib.

Change to St st and join in C (carry yarn not in use neatly up the side of the work).

Proceed as follows:

**Rows 1–4:** Using C, work 4 rows in St st.

**Rows 5–6:** Pick up E and work 2 rows garter st.

Rep the last 6 rows 4 times more, then work rows 1–4 again. Break C and join E.

**Next row:** Knit.

**Next row:** Work in k2, p2 rib.

Work 3 more rows in rib and bind off.

## Sweater front

Use separate balls of red and navy yarns while working the anchor and stripe pattern.

Using size 6/4mm needles and E, cast on 42 sts.

Work 6 rows in k2, p2 rib.

Change to St st and join in C (carry yarn not in use neatly up the side of the work).

Proceed as follows:

**Rows 1–4:** Using C, work 4 rows in St st.

**Rows 5–6:** Pick up E and work 2 rows garter st.

Rep rows 1–6 once more.

Then work rows 1–4 again.

Work anchor motif as follows and *at the same time* maintain the 6-row stripe pattern:

**Row 1:** K16 E, work row 1 of 10-stitch chart over next 10 sts, k16 E.

Cont to work from chart until row 9 is completed. Break D.

Now work in stripe pattern as before over all sts and complete to match back.

## Sleeves
### make 2

Using size 6/4mm needles and E, cast on 42 sts.

Work 6 rows in k2, p2 rib.

Change to St st and join in C (carry yarn not in use neatly up the side of the work).

Proceed as follows:

**Rows 1–4:** Using C, work 4 rows in St st.

**Rows 5–6:** Pick up E and work 2 rows garter st.

Rep rows 1–6 twice more then rows 1–4 again.

Bind off.

## Assembly

Overlap rib on shoulders from front to back for ¾"/2cm on each side. Sew together to form a boat neck. Fold one sleeve in half and mark the center point. Lay the sweater out flat and pin center point of sleeve to shoulder join. Join sleeve to sweater on back and front, making sure each side is equal. Do the same with the other sleeve. Now join side and sleeve seams, matching the stripes.

**ANCHOR CHART (16 sts x 9 rows)**

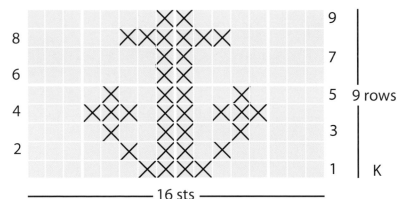

9 rows

16 sts

### Key to chart

X = D

☐ = C

# Cap

Using size 6/4mm needles and E, cast on 54 sts.

Work 5 rows in garter st.

Change to C.

Work 4 rows in St st.

**Next row:** K1, *k1, inc in next st; rep from * to last st, k1 (80 sts).

**Next row:** Purl.

Work 10 rows St st.

**Decrease for the crown**

**Row 1:** *K8, k2tog; rep from * to end of row (72 sts).

**Row 2 and following alt rows:** Purl.

**Row 3:** *K7, k2tog; rep from * to end of row (64 sts).

**Row 5:** *K6, k2tog; rep from * to end of row (56 sts).

Cont decreasing as set, working 1 fewer stitch in each rep until you have reached the row * K1, K2tog, rep from * to end of row.

**Next Row:** Purl.

**Next Row:** K2tog across row.

Break yarn and run through sts on needle, draw up tight and secure.

## Peak

Using size 6/4mm needles and E, cast on 15 sts.

Work 6 rows in garter st.

**Next row:** K2tog at each end of the row (13 sts).

Repeat last row until you have 7 sts.

Bind off.

## Assembly

Join side seam on cap, sew peak to center front.

# Neckerchief

Using size 6/4mm needles and D, cast on 3 sts.

**Row 1:** Knit.

**Row 2:** Inc in first and last st (5 sts).

**Row 3:** Knit (5 sts).

**Row 4:** K2, p1, k2.

**Row 5:** K2, m1, k1, m1, k2 (7 sts).

**Row 6:** K2, p3, k2.

**Row 7:** K2, m1, k3, m1, k2 (9 sts).

**Row 8:** K2, p5, k2.

Cont to inc 1 st at each end of every other row until you have 38 sts.

Work 4 rows even, maintaining the k2 borders on each side as before.

Divide for the neck ties as follows:

**Next row:** Knit.

**Next row:** K2, p6, knit to last 8 sts, p6, k2.

**Next row:** Knit.

**Next row:** K2, p4, k2, bind off center 22 sts, k2, p4, k2.

Proceed on the first set of 8 sts for tie.

**Next row:** K8.

**Next row:** K2, p4, k2.

Rep last 2 rows 9 times more.

**Next row:** K2, skpo, k2tog, k2 (6 sts).

**Next row:** K2, p2, k2.

**Next row:** K6.

**Next row:** K2, p2, k2.

**Next row:** K2, k2tog, k2 (5 sts).

**Next row:** Knit.

Work 12 rows garter st on these sts.

**Next row:** K2tog, k1, k2tog (3 sts).

**Next row:** Knit.

**Next row:** K3tog and fasten off.

Return to remaining set of sts and complete to match first side.

## Finishing

Using white yarn, work "spots" in a random pattern onto the neckerchief with French knots (see page 32).

# Princess Gracie

Every toy box needs a princess, so why not make Gracie, a special teddy bear with her very own sparkly crown and dress? Knitted in a cozy yarn that is so soft to touch, she will be a pleasure to cuddle.

• • • • • • • • • • • • • • • • • • • • • • • • • • • • • • • • • • • • • • • • • • • • • • • • • • • • • • •

## YOU WILL NEED

### For Princess Gracie

Bulky weight (CYCA #6) yarn: (A)
150g (approximately 195 yds) in white
Small amount of brown DK yarn (B)
Scraps of brown fingering yarn for features

*Shown in:*
Bergère de France Plume, 47% polyamide,
42% acrylic, 11% wool (65 yds/60m per 50g ball):
3 x 50g balls in 24793 Tulle

Needles size 9/5.5mm
Needles size 6/4mm
Quality polyester stuffing

### For the dress and crown

DK/Light worsted weight (CYCA #3) yarn:
50g (approximately 186 yds) in pink (C)
Heavy worsted weight (CYCA #4) eyelash:
50g (approximately 87 yds) in metallic pink (D)
Small amount of fingering weight yarn in gold (E)

*Shown in:*
1 x 50g ball Wendy Peter Pan DK  shade 928
1 x 50g ball Wendy Chic in shade pink and silver
Small amount of Twilleys Gold Fingering Yarn
shade Gold for crown

Needles size 6/4mm
Needles size 3/3.25mm
Ribbon roses, ribbon bows,
and narrow matching ribbon

## KNITTING NOTES

### Gauge

15 sts x 20 rows to 4"/10cm for bulky yarn using
size 9/5.5mm needles.
24 sts and 32 rows to 4"/10cm for DK using
size 6/4mm needles.

### Yarn notes

This bear is worked entirely in garter stitch.

### Measurements

12"/30cm tall when sitting. Circumference of belly
when stuffed is about 14"/35.5cm.

### Abbreviations

See page 33.

# Princess Gracie

### Head

Using size 9/5.5mm needles and A, cast on 42 sts.

Knit 4 rows.

**Next row:** K2tog at beg and end of row (40 sts).

Knit 2 rows.

Rep last 3 rows until 4 sts remain.

**Next row:** K2tog twice (2 sts).

**Next row:** K2tog and fasten off.

### Muzzle

Using size 9/5.5mm needles and A, cast on 10 sts.

Inc 1 st at each end of next 2 rows.

Cast on 2 sts at beg of next 2 rows.

Knit 6 rows straight.

Bind off 2 sts at beg of next 2 rows.

K2tog at each end of next 3 rows.

Knit 2 rows and then bind off.

### Body
#### make 2

Using size 9/5.5mm needles and A, cast on 16 sts.

Knit 4 rows.

Inc 1 st at each end of next and following alt rows until you have 26 sts.

Knit 36 rows.

Dec 1 st at each end of next and following alt rows until 14 sts remain.

Bind off. (This is the neck edge.)

### Arms
#### make 2

Using size 9/5.5mm needles and A, cast on 8 sts.

Knit 1 row.

**Next row:** Inc in each stitch across row (16 sts).

Knit 2 rows.

Inc 1 st at each end of next and alt rows until you have 22 sts.

Knit 28 rows.

**Decrease for top of arm**

**Next row:** K2tog at each end of row.

**Next row:** Knit.

Repeat last 2 rows once more.

Bind off. (This is the top of the arm.)

### Legs
#### make 2

Using size 9/5.5mm needles and A, cast on 18 sts.

Knit 1 row.

**Next row:** Inc 1 st in each stitch across row (36 sts).

Knit 16 rows.

**Next row:** K14, k2tog 4 times, k14 (32 sts).

**Next row:** Knit.

**Next row:** K14, k2tog twice, k14 (30 sts).

Knit 26 rows.

**Next row:** K2tog at each end of row (28 sts).

**Next row:** Knit.

**Next row:** K2tog across row (14 sts).

Bind off.

### Outer ears
#### make 2

Using size 9/5.5mm needles and A, cast on 8 sts.

Knit 1 row.

Inc 1 st at each end of next 5 rows (18 sts).

Work 4 rows straight.

**Next row:** K2tog across row (9 sts).

Bind off.

## Inner ears

**make 2**

Work as outer ears but use B instead of A and size 6/4mm needles.

## Assembly

Follow the diagrams at right for sewing the head together. Fold the three points of the triangle to the center, sew along the top dotted lines on each side, then sew along the other dotted line to the chin. Stuff the head to a pleasing shape. Sew the ears together in pairs of one inner and one outer, then attach on each side of the head, curling them slightly when stitching. Stitch the muzzle in place on the head, stuffing lightly to shape. Embroider eyes, nose, and mouth with brown yarn, using the photographs as a guide.

Sew the two body sections together, leaving the neck edge open for stuffing. Stuff firmly and shape, then close the opening. Sew up the arms. The seams should be at the center back, leaving the top open for stuffing and shaping. After stuffing, close the opening. Sew the leg seams but leave the top of the leg open. Stuff and shape, then close the opening. Attach the arms and legs firmly to the body, arranging the teddy in a sitting position.

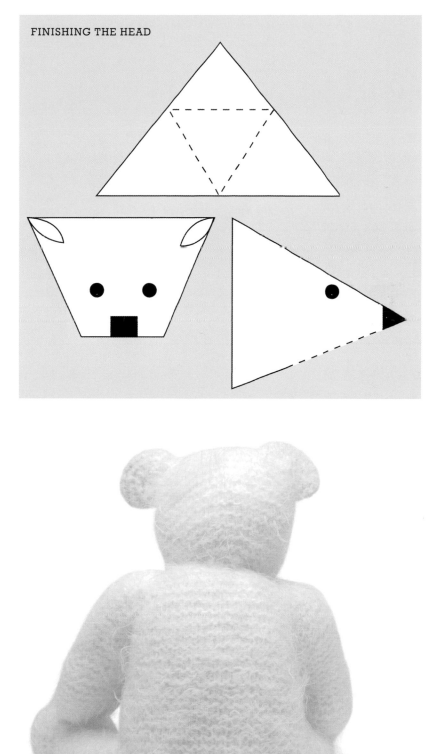

FINISHING THE HEAD

# Dress & crown

## Dress

### make 2

Using size 6/4mm needles and C, cast on 36 sts.

Work in St st for 8 rows.

### Shape armholes

Bind off 3 sts at beg of next 2 rows (30 sts).

**Next row:** K2, skpo, knit to last 4 sts, k2tog, k2 (28 sts).

**Next row:** K2, purl to last 2 sts, k2. Repeat last 2 rows twice more (24 sts).

**Next row:** K2, skpo, knit to last 4 sts, k2tog, k2 (22 sts).

Knit 3 rows in garter stitch.

### Divide for neck and straps

**Next row:** K5, bind off 12 sts, k5. Cont on first set of 5 sts for straps. Work in garter stitch for 14 rows and bind off. Return to remaining 5 sts and work to match first strap.

### Work skirt as follows

With right side facing and using size 6/4mm needles and C, pick up and knit 36 sts from cast-on edge.

**Next row:** Knit.

**Next row (ribbon hole row):** K1, *yo, k2tog; rep from * to last st, k1.

**Next row:** Knit.

**Next row:** Knit, inc 1 st in each st across row (72 sts).

**Next row:** Purl, inc in first and last sts (74 sts).

### Begin lacy pattern:

**Row 1:** K1, *(k2tog) 3 times, (yo, k1) 6 times, (k2tog) 3 times; rep from * to last st, k1.

**Row 2:** Knit.

**Row 3:** Change to D, knit.

**Row 4:** Using D, purl.

**Row 5:** Using C, repeat row 1.

**Row 6:** Knit.

**Row 7:** Knit.

**Row 8:** Purl.

These 8 rows form pattern.

Repeat these 8 rows 3 more times.

Work 4 rows in garter stitch using D. Bind off.

## Assembly

Join the side seams, matching the pattern. Sew the shoulder strap seams. Thread a length of ribbon through the holes at the waist. Add ribbons and roses as in the photos. Slip the dress onto the bear and then tie the ribbon at the waist to gather up the skirt of the dress.

## Crown

### Points of crown (make 5)

Use two strands of yarn knitted together for these points.

Using size 3/3.25mm needles and E, cast on 2 sts.

**Next row:** Knit.

**Next row:** Inc in first st, k1 (3 sts).

**Next row:** Knit.

**Next row:** Inc in first and last sts (5 sts).

**Next row:** Knit.

Cont to inc at each end of next and following alt row (9 sts).

**Next row:** Knit.

Slip sts onto stitch holder.

Make 4 more points in the same way, slipping each point onto the stitch holder.

### Base of crown (Use single strand of yarn)

Using size 3/3.25mm needles and E, knit across each point from stitch holder (45 sts).

**Next row:** Purl.

**Next row:** Knit.

Now work 4 rows in garter st and bind off.

## Finishing

Sew in the ends carefully. Join the short ends of the piece. Now thread a needle with some metallic yarn and sew the points together at the base so they stand up. Attach to the bear's head.

Big Ted

With his camouflage top and bandanna to match, little adventurers are going to love this tough camo bear. He is ready for an action-packed outing. Simple stitches are used to create him and his clothes, so a novice could easily work this design.

## YOU WILL NEED

### For Big Ted

DK/Light worsted weight (CYCA #3) yarn:
100g (approximately 390 yds) in dark brown (A)
50g (approximately 195 yds) in medium brown (B)
Scraps of black and white DK yarn for features

*Shown in:*
Peter Pan DK, 55% nylon, 45% acrylic
(195 yds/170m per 50g ball):
2 x 50g balls Deep Brown shade 915
1 x 50g ball Peter Pan Mid Brown shade 929

Needles size 6/4mm
Quality polyester stuffing

### For sweater and bandanna

DK/Light worsted weight (CYCA #3) yarn:
50g (approximately 110 yds) in camouflage
colors (C)

*Shown in:*
1 x 50g ball West Yorkshire Spinners
Aire Valley, 75% British wool, 25% nylon
(109 yds/100m per 50g) Shade 814

Needles size 6/4mm

## KNITTING NOTES

### Gauge

24 sts and 32 rows to 4"/10cm using size 6/4mm needles.

### Yarn notes

Random-dyed camouflage yarn is used for the bandanna and sweater, but dark green yarn would work just as well.

### Measurements

12"/30cm tall when sitting. Circumference of belly when stuffed is about 13¾"/35cm.

### Abbreviations

See page 33.

# Big Ted
## Body and head
### made in one piece

Using size 6/4mm needles and A, cast on 20 sts.

**Next row:** Purl.

**Next row:** Inc in each st across row (40 sts).

**Next row:** Purl.

**Next row:** *K1, inc in next st; rep from * to end of row (60 sts).

Cont in St st for 44 more rows.

### Decrease row (mark this row for neck of bear)

**Next row:** *K4, skpo; rep from * to end of row (50 sts).

**Next row:** Purl.

Work 26 more rows in St st.

### Shape top of head

**Next row:** *K5, skpo; rep from * to last st, k1 (43 sts).

**Next and following alt (WS) rows:** Purl.

**Next RS row:** *K4, skpo; rep from * to last st, k1 (36 sts).

**Next RS row:** *K3, skpo; rep from * to last st, k1 (29 sts).

**Next RS row:** *K2, skpo; rep from * to last st, k1 (22 sts).

**Next RS row:** *K1, skpo; rep from * to last st, k1 (15 sts).

**Next RS row:** Skpo; rep to last st, k1 (8 sts).

Purl 1 row and bind off.

## Muzzle

Using size 6/4mm needles and B, cast on 10 sts.

**Next row:** Purl.

**Next row:** Inc in each st across row (20 sts).

**Next row:** Purl.

**Next row:** *K1, inc in next st; rep from * to end of row (30 sts).

**Next row:** Purl.

**Next row:** *K2, inc in next st; rep from * to end of row (40 sts).

**Next row:** Purl.

**Next row:** *K3, inc in next st; rep from * to end of row (50 sts).

**Next row:** Purl.

**Next row:** *K4, inc in next st; rep from * to end of row (60 sts).

**Next row:** Purl.

Work 4 rows in St st and bind off.

## Ears
### make 4
Using size 6/4mm needles and B, cast on 10 sts.

Work in St st for 2 rows.

**Next row:** Inc in each st across row (20 sts).

Beg with a purl row, work 9 rows in St st.

**Next row:** K2tog across row (10 sts).

**Next row:** Purl.

**Next row:** K2tog across row (5 sts) and bind off.

## Arms
### make 2
Using size 6/4mm needles and A, cast on 10 sts.

**Next row:** Purl.

**Next row:** *K1, inc in next st; rep from * to end of row (15 sts).

**Next row:** Purl.

**Next row:** *K1, inc in next st; rep from * to last st, k1 (22 sts).

**Next row:** Purl.

**Next row:** Inc in first and last st (24 sts).

Beg with a purl row, work 27 rows in St st.

**Next row:** *K1, skpo; rep from * to end of row (16 sts).

**Next row:** Purl.

**Next row:** K2tog across row (8 sts).

**Next row:** Purl.

**Next row:** K2tog across row (4 sts). Break yarn and run through sts left on needle. Draw up and fasten off.

## Legs
### make 2
Using size 6/4mm needles and A, cast on 10 sts.

**Next row:** Purl.

**Next row:** *K1, inc in next st; rep from * to end of row (15 sts).

**Next row:** Purl.

**Next row:** *K1, inc in next st; rep from * to last st, k1 (22 sts).

**Next row:** Purl.

**Next row:** Inc in first and last st (24 sts).

**Next row:** Purl.

Repeat last 2 rows once more (26 sts).

Cont in St st for 24 rows.

### Increase for foot
**Next row:** K9, inc in each of next 8 sts, k9 (34 sts).

**Next row:** Purl.

**Next row:** K12, inc in each of next 10 sts, k12 (44 sts).

Beg with a purl row, work 9 rows St st.

**Next row:** K2tog across row (22 sts).

**Next row:** Purl.

**Next row:** K2tog across row (11 sts).

**Next row:** Purl.

**Next row:** K2tog across row to last st, k1 (6 sts).

Break yarn and run through sts left on needle. Draw up and fasten off.

## Nose

Using size 6/4mm needles and A, cast on 8 sts.

Work 4 rows in St st.

**Next row:** K2tog, work to last 2 sts, k2tog (6 sts).

**Next row:** Purl.

**Next row:** K2tog, k2, k2tog (4 sts).

**Next row:** Purl.

**Next row:** K2tog twice (2 sts).

**Next row:** Purl.

**Next row:** K2tog and fasten off. Leave a long tail of yarn to form the mouth.

## Assembly

Begin with the head and body of the bear. Sew the back seam, which runs down the back of the bear, leaving the base open to stuff.

Stuff the head first, making it firm and round. Thread a needle with matching yarn and, beginning at the marked row for the neck, weave the yarn in and out of each stitch all the way around, beginning and ending at the seam. Pull up firmly to form the head and neck. Secure well at the seam. Continue to stuff the body, then close the base.

Sew the side seam of the muzzle to form a cup shape, add some stuffing, and then pin it to the front of the head using the photos as a guide. Sew the muzzle in place.

Pin the nose in the center of the muzzle, with the widest part at the top. Add a bit of stuffing to pad it out slightly, then sew in place. Use the long tail of yarn left and stitch to the base of the muzzle, pulling it firmly to form the bear's mouth.

Embroider the eyes using black and white yarn. Sew the ears together in pairs and attach to each side of the head. Sew the arm seams, leaving the tops open for stuffing. Stuff and attach the arms to the shoulders on each side.

Sew the leg seams and stuff, filling out the feet for a nice shape. Sew the legs to each side of the bear in a sitting position.

# Sweater & bandanna

### Sweater body

**make 2**

Using size 6/4mm needles and C, cast on 36 sts.

Work 6 rows in k2, p2 rib.

Change to St st and work 30 rows.

Work 6 rows k2, p2 rib.

Bind off.

### Sleeves

**make 2**

Using size 6/4mm needles and C, cast on 30 sts.

Work 5 rows in k2, p2 rib.

Change to St st and work 20 rows.

Bind off.

## Assembly

Sew the shoulder seams of the sweater body back and front, overlapping the rib from front to back on each side for ¾"/2cm to form the envelope neck. Sew the sleeves in position on each side, then sew the underarm and side seams. Slip onto the bear.

### Bandanna

**worked in garter stitch**

Using size 6/4mm needles and C, cast on 2 sts.

**Next row:** K1, inc in next st (3 sts).

**Next row:** Knit.

** **Next row:** Inc in first and last st (5 sts).

**Next row:** Knit.

**Next row:** Inc in first and last st (7 sts).

**Next row:** Knit. **

Knit 16 rows.

K2tog at each end of next and following alt rows (3 sts).

Knit 5 rows.

Work from ** to ** (7 sts).

Cont in garter stitch until strip is long enough to fit around bear's head.

**Next row:** K2tog at each end of row.

**Next row:** Knit.

Repeat last 2 rows until you have 3 sts.

Knit 5 rows.

Inc 1 st at each end of next and following alt rows to 7 sts.

Knit 16 rows.

K2tog at each end of next and following alt rows to 3 sts.

**Next row:** K3tog and fasten off. Sew in yarn ends and tie around bear's head.

Patches

With his endearing expression and checkered shirt, this country bear is all set to melt your heart. Worked in stockinette stitch and garter stitch he is very simple to make. The shirt is embroidered using chain stitch, but it could also be left plain or striped.

● ● ● ● ● ● ● ● ● ● ● ● ● ● ● ● ● ● ● ● ● ● ● ● ● ● ● ● ● ● ● ● ● ● ● ● ● ● ● ● ● ● ● ● ● ● ● ●

## YOU WILL NEED

### For Patches

DK/Light worsted weight (CYCA #3) yarn:
100g (approximately 309 yds) in light brown (A)

*Shown in:*
Bergère de France Norvège, 40% wool, 40% acrylic, 20% mohair (154 yds/140m per 50g ball): 2 x 50g balls in 31126 Duvet

Needles size 6/4mm
Needles size 7/4.5mm
Quality polyester stuffing

### For the top and dungarees

DK/Light worsted weight (CYCA #3) yarn:
50g (approximately 179 yds) each in cream (B), blue (C), and red (D)
Scraps of medium brown, black and white DK yarn for nose and features

*Shown in:*
Sirdar Snuggly DK, 55% nylon, 45% acrylic (179 yds/164m per 50g):
1 x 50g ball Cream shade 203
1 x 50g ball Denim Blue shade 326
1 x 50g ball Cherry Pie Shade 437

Needles size 6/4mm
Shirring elastic

## KNITTING NOTES

### Gauge

20 sts and 26 rows to 4"/10cm for mohair using size 7/4.5mm needles.
22 sts and 28 rows to 4"/10cm for DK using size 6/4mm needles.

### Yarn notes

You may substitute this yarn for a similar weight DK yarn that gives the same gauge.

### Measurements

11"/28cm tall when sitting. Circumference of belly when stuffed is about 15"/38cm.

### Abbreviations

See page 33.

## Muzzle

Using size 7/4.5mm needles and A, cast on 10 sts.

**Next row:** Purl.

**Next row:** Inc in each st across row (20 sts).

**Next row:** Purl.

**Next row:** *K1, inc in next st; rep from * to end of row (30 sts).

**Next row:** Purl.

**Next row:** *K2, inc in next st; rep from * to end of row (40 sts).

**Next row:** Purl.

**Next row:** *K3, inc in next st; rep from * to end of row (50 sts).

**Next row:** Purl.

**Next row:** *K4, inc in next st; rep from * to end of row (60 sts).

**Next row:** Purl.

**Next row:** *K5, inc in next st; rep from * to end of row (70 sts).

Work 6 rows in St st and bind off.

# Patches
## Body and head
### made in one piece

Using size 7/4.5mm needles and A, cast on 20 sts.

**Next row:** Purl.

**Next row:** Inc in each st across row (40 sts).

**Next row:** Purl.

**Next row:** *K1, inc in next st; rep from * to end of row (60 sts).

Cont even in St st for 38 more rows.

**Decrease row (mark this row for neck of bear)**

**Next row:** *K4, skpo; rep from * to end of row (50 sts).

**Next row:** Purl.

Cont even in St st for 26 more rows.

### Shape top of head

**Next row:** *K5, skpo; rep from * to last st, k1 (43 sts).

**Next and following alt rows:** Purl.

**Next RS row:** *K4, skpo; rep from * to last st, k1 (36 sts).

**Next RS row:** *K3, skpo; rep from * to last st, k1 (29 sts).

**Next RS row:** *K2, skpo; rep from * to last st, k1 (22 sts).

**Next RS row:** *K1, skpo; rep from * to last st, k1 (15 sts).

**Next RS row:** Skpo; rep to last st, k1 (8 sts).

Purl 1 row and bind off.

## Right arm

Using size 7/4.5mm needles and A, cast on 10 sts.

**Next row:** Purl.

**Next row:** *K1, inc in next st; rep from * to end of row (15 sts).

**Next row:** Purl.

**Next row:** *K1, inc in next st; rep from * to last st, k1 (22 sts).

**Next row:** Purl.

**Next row:** Inc in first and last st (24 sts).

Beg with a purl row, work 17 rows in St st.

### Shape arm

**Next row:** K12, turn and purl back.

**Next row:** K13, turn and purl back.

**Next row:** K14, turn and purl back.

**Next row:** K15, turn and purl back.

**Next row:** Knit across all sts.

**Next row:** Purl.

Work 8 rows in St st.

**Next row:** *K1, skpo; rep from * to end (16 sts).

**Next row:** Purl.

**Next row:** K2tog across row (8 sts).

**Next row:** Purl.

**Next row:** K2tog across row (4 sts). Break yarn and run through sts left on needle. Draw up and fasten off.

## Left arm

Using size 7/4.5mm needles and A, cast on 10 sts.

**Next row:** Purl.

**Next row:** *K1, inc in next st; rep from * to end of row (15 sts).

**Next row:** Purl.

**Next row:** *K1, inc in next st; rep from * to last st, k1 (22 sts).

**Next row:** Purl.

**Next row:** Inc in first and last st (24 sts).

Beg with a purl row, work 18 rows in St st.

## Shape arm

**Next row:** P12, turn and knit back.

**Next row:** P13, turn and knit back.

**Next row:** P14, turn and knit back.

**Next row:** P15, turn and knit back.

**Next row:** Purl across all sts.

Work 8 rows in St st.

**Next row:** *K1, skpo; rep from * to end (16 sts).

**Next row:** Purl.

**Next row:** K2tog across row (8 sts).

**Next row:** Purl.

**Next row:** K2tog across row (4 sts) Break yarn and run through sts left on needle. Draw up and fasten off.

## Legs
### make 2

Using size 7/4.5mm needles and A, cast on 10 sts.

**Next row:** Purl.

**Next row:** *K1, inc in next st; rep from * to end of row (15 sts).

**Next row:** Purl.

**Next row:** *K1, inc in next st; rep from * to last st, k1 (22 sts).

**Next row:** Purl.

**Next row:** Inc in first and last st (24 sts).

**Next row:** Purl.

Repeat last 2 rows once more (26 sts).

Cont in St st for 24 rows.

**Increase for foot**

**Next row:** K9, inc in each of next 8 sts, k9 (34 sts).

Beg with a purl row, work 11 rows St st.

**Next row:** K2tog across row (17 sts).

**Next row:** Purl.

**Next row:** K2tog across row to last st, k1 (9 sts).

**Next row:** Purl.

Break yarn and run through sts left on needle. Draw up and fasten off.

## Ears
### make 4

Using size 7/4.5mm needles and A, cast on 8 sts.

Work in St st for 4 rows.

**Next:** Inc 1 st at each end of next and following alt rows until you have 14 sts, ending on a purl row. Work 8 rows St st.

**Next row:** K2tog across row (7 sts). Bind off.

## Nose
### worked in garter stitch

Using size 6/4mm needles and medium brown DK yarn, cast on 3 sts and knit 1 row.

**Next row:** Inc in first and last st (5 sts).

**Next row:** Knit.

Repeat last 2 rows once more (7 sts).

Knit 6 rows without shaping.

**Next row:** K2tog at each end of row (5 sts).

**Next row:** Knit.

Repeat last 2 rows once more. Knit 1 row and bind off.

## Assembly

Sew the head and body seam, which runs down the back of the bear, leaving the base open to stuff. Stuff the head first, making it firm and round. Using a needle threaded with matching yarn, and beginning at the marked row for the neck, weave the yarn in and out of each stitch all the way around, beginning and ending at the seam. Pull up firmly to form the head and neck. Secure well at the seam. Continue to stuff the body, then close the base.

Sew the side seam of the muzzle to form a cup shape. Add some stuffing then pin to the front of the bear's head, using the photos as a guide. Sew the muzzle in place. Pin the nose in the center of the muzzle, so that the longest sides are at the top and bottom. Sew the nose in place. Embroider the eyes and eyebrows using black and white yarn. Sew the ears together in pairs and attach to either side of the head.

Sew the seams on the arms, leaving the top open for stuffing, then stuff and attach to the bear's shoulders on either side.

Sew the leg seams and stuff, making sure that you fill out the feet to give a nice shape. Sew the legs to each side of the bear in a sitting position.

# Dungarees
## Front

**** Begin with first leg.

** Using size 6/4mm needles and C, cast on 23 sts.

Work 2 rows in garter stitch.

Change to St st and work 26 rows.**

### Inc for crotch

**Next row:** Inc 1 st at beginning of row, knit to end.

**Next row:** Purl to last st, inc in st.

Rep last 2 rows 2 times more (29 sts).

Leave stitches on a spare needle for now.

### Work second leg

Work as first leg from ** to **.

**Next row:** Knit to last st, inc in st.

**Next row:** Inc in first stitch, purl to end.

Repeat last 2 rows 2 times more.

To join two sets of stitches together, knit across stitches on needle, then knit across stitches on spare needle (58 sts).

Beg with a purl row, work 21 rows in St st on these sts.

Change to k1, p1 rib and work 6 rows. ****

### Begin bib

**Next row:** Bind off 20 sts, k18, bind off 20 sts. Break yarn.

Rejoin yarn to remaining sts and proceed as follows:

**Next row:** K2, purl to last 2 sts, k2.

**Next row:** Knit.

**Next row:** K2, purl to last 2 sts, k2.
Repeat last 2 rows 5 times more.
Knit 4 rows garter stitch across
all stitches.
**Next row:** K4, bind off 10 sts, k4.
Proceed on first set of 4 sts
for strap.
Knit 46 rows garter stitch and
bind off.
Rejoin yarn to remaining stitches
and work to match first side.

## Back

Work as for front from **** to ****
and bind off in rib.

## Patch

Using size 6/4mm needles and D,
cast on 10 sts.
Work in St st for 14 rows and
bind off.

## Assembly

Join the side seams and underleg
seams. Using some elastic and a
blunt-ended needle, thread elastic
through the last 3 rows of the rib on
the back of the dungarees at waist
level. Draw in firmly to take up
fullness but maintain elasticity.
Fasten off firmly. Join the straps to the
back edge of the dungarees. Stitch
the patch to one of the legs using a
contrast yarn and large stitches.

# Top

## Back

Using size 6/4mm needles and B,
cast on 37 sts.
Work 3 rows garter stitch.
Change to St st and stripe pattern.
Work 4 rows St st in B.
Join D yarn.
Work 2 rows St st.
Repeat last 6 rows 5 times more.
Knit 4 rows St st in B.
Work 3 rows garter stitch and
bind off.

## Front

Work as back until 4th D stripe is
completed.

**Divide for neck**
**Next row:** Knit 18, bind off 1 st,
k18. Proceed on first set of 18 sts for
right front neck.
**Next row:** Purl to last 2 sts, k2.
**Next row:** Knit.
**Next row:** Purl to last 2 sts, k2.
**Next row:** Using D, knit.
**Next row:** Using D, purl to last 2
sts, k2.
**Next row:** Using B, bind off 6 sts,
knit to end of row.
**Next row:** Purl to last st, k1.
Continue on these sts, keeping
stripe pattern as established and
1 st in garter stitch at neck edge,
until work matches back.
Work 4 rows garter stitch and
bind off.

Rejoin yarn to sts left and work
to match other side, reversing
shapings.

## Sleeves
**make 2**

Using size 6/4mm needles
and B, cast on 31 sts.
Work 3 rows garter stitch.
Change to St st and stripe pattern.
Work 4 rows St st with B.
Join D yarn.
Work 2 rows St st.
Repeat last 6 rows twice more.
Knit 4 rows St st with B and bind off.

## Assembly

Using D and a blunt-ended needle,
work chain stitch along the vertical
rows of stockinette stitch on each
separate piece of the top. Start from
the center stitch and skip 3 stitches
of stockinette stitch between each
stripe. This is very time consuming
so be patient. Work in the yarn ends
at each stripe.

Sew the shoulder seams for
approx ¾"/2cm, then join the
sleeves to back and fronts on each
side. Sew the side and sleeve
seams matching the stripes. Make
a twisted cord using D and lace
through the fronts to tie the neck.

Pumpkin

Knit this gorgeous Halloween bear to take along with you trick-or-treating. He even has his own scary cape complete with pumpkin motif. Knitted in stockinette stitch, this is a very simple bear to make.

• • • • • • • • • • • • • • • • • • • • • • • • • • • • • • • • • • • • • • • • • • • • • • •

## YOU WILL NEED

### For Pumpkin

DK/Light worsted weight (CYCA #3) yarn:
100g (approximately 340 yds) in orange (A)

*Shown in:*
Sirdar Country Style DK, 40% nylon, 30% wool, 30% acrylic (170 yds/155m per 50g ball):
2 x 50g balls in 618 Snapdragon

Needles size 6/4mm
Needles size 3/3.25mm
Quality polyester stuffing

### For the cape, inner ears and paw pads

DK/Light worsted weight (CYCA #3) yarn:
100g (approximately 340 yds) in black (B)
Small amounts of green and orange fingering weight yarns for pumpkin motif

*Shown in:*
2 x 50g balls Sirdar Country Style DK, 40% nylon, 30% wool, 30% acrylic (170 yds/155m per 50g ball):
2 x 50g balls in 417 Black

Needles size 6/4mm

## KNITTING NOTES

### Gauge

22 sts and 28 rows to 4"/10cm using size 6/4mm needles.

### Yarn notes

Any DK weight yarn will work with this project. Check your gauge and change the needle size if necessary.

### Measurements

10"/26cm tall when sitting. Circumference of belly when stuffed is about 13½"/34.5cm.

### Abbreviations

See page 33.

# Pumpkin

### Head

Using size 6/4mm needles and A, cast on 8 sts.

**Next row:** Purl.

**Next row:** Inc in each st across row (16 sts).

**Next row:** Purl.

**Next row:** K4, m1, k8, m1, k4 (18 sts).

**Next row:** Purl.

**Next row:** K4, m1, k1, m1, k8, m1, k1, m1, k4 (22 sts).

**Next row:** Purl.

**Next row:** K5, m1, k1, m1, k10, m1, k1, m1, k5 (26 sts).

**Next row:** Purl.

Cont increasing in this manner, working 2 more stitches between the 2nd and 3rd increases and working a plain purl row between the increase rows, until you have 66 sts, ending on a purl row.

Work 10 rows in St st decreasing 1 st at each end of row on the final row (64 sts).

**Decrease for back of head**

**Next row:** *K6, k2tog; rep from * to end of row (56 sts).

**Next and following alt rows:** Purl.

**Next RS row:** *K5, k2tog; rep from * to end of row (48 sts).

**Next RS row:** *K4, k2tog; rep from * to end of row (40 sts).

**Next RS row:** *K3, k2tog; rep from * to end of row (32 sts).

**Next RS row:** *K2, k2tog; rep from * to end of row (24 sts).

**Next RS row:** *K1, k2tog; rep from * to end of row (16 sts).

**Next RS row:** K2tog across row (8 sts). Break yarn and run through sts left on needle. Draw up and fasten off.

### Body

Using size 6/4mm needles and A, cast on 20 sts.

**Next row:** Purl.

**Next row:** Inc in each st across row (40 sts).

**Next row:** Purl.

**Next row:** *K1, inc in next st; rep from * to end of row (60 sts).

Cont even in St st until you have worked 57 rows, ending with a purl row.

**Decrease for top of body**

**Next row:** *K4, k2tog; rep from * to end of row (50 sts).

**Next and following alt rows:** Purl.

**Next RS row:** *K3, k2tog; rep from * to end of row (40 sts).

**Next RS row:** *K2, k2tog; rep from * to end of row (30 sts).

**Next RS row:** *K1, k2tog; rep from * to end of row (20 sts).

**Next row:** K2tog across row (10 sts).

Break yarn and run through sts left on needle. Draw up and fasten off.

## Ears

**make 2 in A and 2 in B**

Using size 6/4mm needles and appropriate color, cast on 10 sts.

Work in garter stitch for 2 rows.

Inc in first and last st every alt row to 16 sts.

Work 8 rows garter st.

**Next row:** K2tog across row (8 sts).

**Next row:** Knit.

**Next row:** K2tog across row (4 sts).

Bind off.

## Arms

**make 2**

Using size 6/4mm needles and A, cast on 10 sts.

**Next row:** Purl.

**Next row:** *K1, inc in next st; rep from * to end of row (15 sts).

**Next row:** Purl.

**Next row:** *K1, inc in next st; rep from * to last st, k1 (22 sts).

**Next row:** Purl.

**Next row:** Inc in first and last st (24 sts).

Beg with a purl row, work 27 rows in St st.

**Next row:** *K1, skpo; rep from * to end of row (16 sts).

**Next row:** Purl.

**Next row:** K2tog across row (8 sts).

**Next row:** Purl.

**Next row:** K2tog across row (4 sts).

Break yarn and run through sts left on needle. Draw up and fasten off.

## Legs
### make 2

Using size 6/4mm needles and A, cast on 10 sts.

**Next row:** Purl.

**Next row:** *K1, inc in next st; rep from * to end of row (15 sts).

**Next row:** Purl.

**Next row:** *K1, inc in next st; rep from * to last st, k1 (22 sts).

**Next row:** Purl.

**Next row:** Inc in first and last st (24 sts).

**Next row:** Purl.

Repeat last 2 rows once more (26 sts).

Cont in St st for 24 rows.

### Increase for foot

**Next row:** K9, inc in each of next 8 sts, k9 (34 sts).

**Next row:** Purl.

**Next row:** K12, inc in each of next 10 sts, k12 (44 sts).

Beg with a purl row, work 9 rows St st.

**Next row:** K2tog across row (22 sts).

**Next row:** Purl.

**Next row:** K2tog across row (11 sts).

**Next row:** Purl.

**Next row:** K2tog across row to last st, k1 (6 sts).

Break yarn and run through sts left on needle. Draw up and fasten off.

## Paw pads
### make 2, worked in garter stitch

Using size 6/4mm needles and B, cast on 10 sts.

Knit 10 rows.

**Next row:** K2tog at each end of row (8 sts).

**Next row:** Knit.

Repeat last 2 rows until 4 sts remain.

Bind off.

## Feet pads
### make 2, worked in garter stitch
Using size 6/4mm needles and B, cast on 7 sts.

Knit 2 rows.

Inc 1 st at each end of next and following alt rows until you have 13 sts.

Knit 12 rows.

Dec 1 st at each end of the next and following alt rows until you have 7 sts.

Bind off.

## Nose
Using size 6/4mm needles and B, cast on 8 sts.

Work 6 rows in garter stitch.

Dec 1 st at each end of next and following alt rows to 2 sts.

**Next row:** K2tog, fasten off, leaving a long tail of yarn.

## Assembly
Sew the body seam, which runs down the back, and stuff firmly before closing.

Sew the head seam, stuffing firmly as for the body.

Sew the ears together in pairs, one black and one orange, curling them inward as you go. Sew one to each side of the head.

Pin the nose in place on the bear's face, pad it out a little, and stitch it in place. Using black yarn, embroider the eyes onto the face, tugging them a little to create indentations and add shape to the nose. Attach the bear's head to the body.

Sew the seams on undersides of the arms and legs. Stuff firmly. Sew a pad to each paw and a foot pad to the base of each foot.

Pin the arms and legs in position on the bear so that he is in a sitting position, aligning the legs so the bear will sit evenly. Sew in place.

# Cape

Using size 6/4mm needles and B, cast on 48 sts.

Work 4 rows in garter stitch.

**Next row:** K4, purl to last 4 sts, k4.

**Next row:** Knit.

**Next row:** K4, purl to last 4 sts, k4.
Repeat last 2 rows twice more.

**Next row (make eyelet holes):**
K5, *yo, k2tog, k1; rep from * to last 5 sts, k5.

**Next row:** K4, purl to last 4 sts, k4.
Work 4 rows in St st (dec 1 st on last row) (47 sts).

**Begin to shape cape**

**Next row:** K4, *k9, m1, k1, m1; rep from * to last 13 sts, k13 (53 sts).

**\*\*Next row:** K4, purl to last 4 sts, k4.

**Next row:** Knit.

**Next row:** K4, purl to last 4 sts, k4.\*\*

**Next row:** K14, m1, k1, m1, *k11, m1, k1, m1; rep from * to last 14 sts, k14 (59 sts).
Work from ** to **.

**Next row:** K15, m1, k1, m1, *k13, m1, k1, m1; rep from * to last 15 sts, k15 (65 sts).
Work from ** to **.
Cont to increase in this manner until you have worked the row:
"K18, m1, k1, m1, *k19, m1, k1, m1; rep from * to last 18 sts, k18 (83 sts)."

**Next row:** K4, purl to last 4 sts, k4.

**Next row:** Knit.

**Next row:** K4, purl to last 4 sts, k4.
Repeat last 2 rows 7 times more.
Work 5 rows in garter stitch.
Bind off.

## Finishing

Make a twisted cord using black yarn and thread it through the holes at the neckline. Sew leaves to top of pumpkin. Embroider the eyes and mouth with black yarn. Attach the motif to center back of cape.

## Motif for cape

### Pumpkin

Using size 3/3.25mm needles and orange fingering weight yarn, cast on 10 sts. Knit 2 rows in garter stitch.

Inc 1 st at each end of next and following alt rows to 20 sts.

Work in garter stitch on these sts for 16 rows.

Dec 1 st at beginning and end of next and following alt rows to 14 sts.

Knit 2 rows and bind off.

### Leaves

Using size 3/3.25mm needles and green fingering weight yarn, cast on 2 sts.

**Next row:** Knit.
**\*\*Next row:** Inc in first and last stitch (4 sts).
**Next row:** Knit
Repeat last 2 rows once more (6 sts).
**Next row:** K2tog at each end of next and following alt row (2 sts). \*\*
Knit 2 rows.
Work from \*\* to \*\*.
K2tog and fasten off.

Snowflake

Wrapped up warm in his scarf and earmuffs, this winter bear is ready to join you for a walk in the snow. You don't have to use the color I have chosen for his earmuffs and scarf; instead, why not knit them in your own favorite shades?

## YOU WILL NEED

### For Snowflake

DK/Light worsted weight (CYCA #3) yarn: 200g (approximately 540 yds) in cream (A)

Scraps of black DK yarn for nose and features

*Shown in:*
Jarol Heritage DK, 55% wool, 25% acrylic, 20% nylon (270 yds/250m per 100g ball): 2 x 100g balls in 100 Cream

Needles size 6/4mm
Quality polyester stuffing

### For the scarf and earmuffs

DK/Light worsted weight (CYCA #3) yarn: 50g (approximately 98 yds) in turquoise (B)

*Shown in:*
Patons Diploma Gold DK 100% wool (98 yds/90m per 50g ball): 1 x 50g ball in in 06243 Bright Aqua

Needles size 6/4mm
Pompon maker or small piece of cardboard

## KNITTING NOTES

### Gauge

22 sts and 28 rows to 4"/10cm using size 6/4mm needles.

### Yarn notes

Any DK weight yarn will work with this project. Check your gauge and change needle size if needed.

### Measurements

10"/26cm) tall when sitting. Circumference of belly when stuffed is about 13½"/34.5cm.

### Abbreviations

See page 33.

# Snowflake

## Head

Using size 6/4mm needles and A, cast on 8 sts.

**Next row:** Purl.

**Next row:** Inc in each st across row (16 sts).

**Next row:** Purl.

**Next row:** K4, m1, k8, m1, k4 (18 sts).

**Next row:** Purl.

**Next row:** K4, m1, k1, m1, k8, m1, k1, m1, k4 (22 sts).

**Next row:** Purl.

**Next row:** K5, m1, k1, m1, k10, m1, k1, m1, k5 (26 sts).

**Next row:** Purl.

Cont increasing in this manner, working 2 more stitches between the 2nd and 3rd increases and working a plain purl row between the increase rows, until you have 66 sts, ending on a purl row.

Work 10 rows in St st decreasing 1 st at each end of row on the final row (64 sts).

### Decrease for back of head

**Next row:** *K6, k2tog; rep from * to end of row (56 sts).

Next and following alt rows, purl.

**Next RS row:** *K5, k2tog; rep from * to end of row (48 sts).

**Next RS row:** *K4, k2tog; rep from * to end of row (40 sts).

**Next RS row:** *K3, k2tog; rep from * to end of row (32 sts).

**Next RS row:** *K2, k2tog; rep from * to end of row (24 sts).

**Next RS row:** *K1, k2tog; rep from * to end of row (16 sts).

**Next RS row:** K2tog across row (8 sts).

Break yarn and run through sts left on needle. Draw up and fasten off.

## Body

Using size 6/4mm needles and A, cast on 20 sts.

**Next row:** Purl.

**Next row:** Inc in each st across row (40 sts).

**Next row:** Purl.

**Next row:** *K1, inc in next st; rep from * to end of row (60 sts).

Cont even in St st for 46 more rows.

**Decrease for top of body**

**Next row:** *K4, k2tog; rep from * to end of row (50 sts).

**Next and following alt rows:** Purl.

**Next RS row:** *K3, k2tog; rep from * to end of row (40 sts).

**Next RS row:** *K2, k2tog; rep from * to end of row (30 sts).

**Next RS row:** *K1, k2tog; rep from * to end of row (20 sts).

**Next row:** K2tog across row (10 sts).

Break yarn and run through sts left on needle. Draw up and fasten off.

## Ears
### make 4

Using size 6/4mm needles and A, cast on 10 sts.

Beg with knit work 2 rows St st.

Inc in first and last st on every alt row to 16 sts.

Beg with a purl row, work 5 rows in St st.

**Next row:** K2tog across row (8 sts)

**Next row:** Purl.

**Next row:** K2tog across row (4 sts). Bind off.

## Right arm

Using size 6/4mm needles and A, cast on 10 sts.

**Next row:** Purl.

**Next row:** *K1, inc in next st; rep from * to end of row (15 sts).

**Next row:** Purl.

**Next row:** *K1, inc in next st; rep from * to last st, k1 (22 sts).

**Next row:** Purl.

**Next row:** Inc in first and last st (24 sts).

Beg with a purl row, work 17 rows in St st.

**Shape arm**

**Next row:** K12, turn and purl back.

**Next row:** K13, turn and purl back.

**Next row:** K14, turn and purl back.

**Next row:** K15, turn and purl back.

**Next row:** Knit across all sts.

**Next row:** Purl.

Work 8 rows in St st.

**Next row:** *K1, skpo; rep from * to end of row (16 sts).

**Next row:** Purl.

**Next row:** K2tog across row (8 sts).

**Next row:** Purl.

Break yarn and run through sts left on needle. Draw up and fasten off.

## Legs
### make 2

Using size 6/4mm needles and A, cast on 10 sts.

**Next row:** Purl.

**Next row:** *K1, inc in next st; rep from * to end of row (15 sts).

**Next row:** Purl.

**Next row:** *K1, inc in next st; rep from * to last st, k1 (22 sts).

**Next row:** Purl.

**Next row:** Inc in first and last st (24 sts).

**Next row:** Purl.

Repeat last 2 rows once more (26 sts).

Cont in St st for 24 rows.

**Increase for foot**

**Next row:** K9, inc in each of next 8 sts, k9 (34 sts).

**Next row:** Purl.

**Next row:** K12, inc in each of next 10 sts, k12 (44 sts).

Beg with a purl row, work 9 rows St st.

**Next row:** K2tog across row (22 sts).

**Next row:** Purl.

**Next row:** K2tog across row (11 sts).

**Next row:** Purl.

**Next row:** K2tog across row to last st, k1 (6 sts).

Break yarn and run through sts left on needle. Draw up and fasten off.

## Left arm

Using size 6/4mm needles and A, cast on 10 sts.

**Next row:** Purl.

**Next row:** *K1, inc in next st; rep from * to end of row (15 sts).

**Next row:** Purl.

**Next row:** *K1, inc in next st; rep from * to last st, k1 (22 sts).

**Next row:** Purl.

**Next row:** Inc in first and last st (24 sts).

Beg with a purl row, work 18 rows in St st.

## Shape arm

**Next row:** P12, turn and knit back.

**Next row:** P13, turn and knit back.

**Next row:** P14, turn and knit back.

**Next row:** P15, turn and knit back.

**Next row:** Purl across all sts.

Now work 8 rows in St st.

**Next row:** *K1, skpo; rep from * to end of row (16 sts).

**Next row:** Purl.

**Next row:** K2tog across row (8 sts).

**Next row:** Purl.

**Next row:** K2tog across row (4 sts).

Break yarn and run through sts left on needle. Draw up and fasten off.

## Nose

Using size 6/4mm needles and black yarn, cast on 8 sts.
Work 4 rows in St st.
**Next row:** K2tog, knit to last 2 sts, K2tog (6 sts).
**Next row:** Purl.
**Next row:** K2tog, k2, k2tog (4 sts).
**Next row:** Purl
**Next row:** K2tog twice.
**Next row:** Purl.
**Next row:** K2tog and fasten off.
Leave a long tail of yarn to use for the bear's mouth.

## Assembly

Sew seam on body, which runs down the back, and stuff firmly before closing. Sew seam on the head, stuffing firmly.

Sew the ears together in pairs, curling them inward as you sew. Sew the ears to each side of the head.

Pin the nose in place on the bear's face, padding it out a little with stuffing before stitching in place. Using some black yarn, embroider the eyes. Tug them a little to create indentations and add shape to the nose. Attach the head to the body.

Sew the seams on the arms and legs. Stuff firmly.

Pin the limbs in position on the bear in a sitting position; be sure the seams run on the underside. Position the limbs equally so the bear sits evenly. Sew the arms and legs in place.

# Scarf

Using size 6/4mm needles and B, cast on 13 sts.

Work 4 rows garter stitch.

**Begin pattern**

**Row 1:** K6, p1, K6.

**Row 2:** K3, p3, k1, p3, k3.

Repeat last 2 rows once and then row 1 again.

**Next row:** Knit.

These 6 rows form pattern.

Rep 5 times more.

**Next row:** K4, k2tog, k1, k2tog, k4 (11 sts).

**Next row:** Knit.

**Next row:** K3, k2tog 3 times, k2 (8 sts).

**Next row:** Knit.

**Next row:** K2, k2tog twice, k2 (6 sts).

Knit 60 rows.

**Next row:** K2, inc in each of next 2 sts, k2 (8 sts).

**Next row:** Knit.

**Next row:** K3, inc in each of next 3 sts, k2 (11 sts).

**Next row:** Knit.

**Next row:** K4, inc in next st, k1, inc in next st, k4 (13 sts).

**Next row:** Knit.

**Begin pattern**

**Row 1:** K6, p1, K6.

**Row 2:** K3, p3, k1, p3, k3.

Rep last 2 rows once and then row 1 again.

**Next row:** Knit.

These 6 rows form pattern.

Repeat pattern rows 5 times more.

Work 4 rows in garter stitch and bind off.

Work in the yarn ends, then wrap scarf around the bear's neck.

# Earmuffs

### make 2, worked in garter stitch

Using size 6/4mm needles and B, cast on 4 sts.

Knit 2 rows.

**Next row:** Inc in first and last stitch (6 sts).

**Next row:** Knit.

Rep last 2 rows once more (8 sts).

Knit 6 rows.

**Next row:** K2tog at each end of row (6 sts).

**Next row:** Knit.

Rep last 2 rows once more (4 sts).

Knit 2 rows and bind off.

## Headband

Using size 6/4mm needles and B, cast on 28 sts.

Knit 3 rows and bind off.

## Assembly

To assemble the earmuffs, join one circle to each end of the headband. Make two pompons (see below) and trim to a neat shape. Sew one to each of the circles. Tack the headband in place over the top of the head.

Pompons can be made using a pompon maker, or they can be made in the traditional way using two circles of cardboard with a hole cut out of the centers, winding the yarn around the card until the center circle is full. Cut the yarn between the two pieces of cardboard and pass a length of yarn into the same place and tie it tightly. Pull the cardboard away from the resulting pompon, and trim it to a neat shape.

Lily

Celebrate a special birthday with this sweet teddy bear! Knitted in a soft furry yarn and with a pretty dress complete with heart motif, Lily will be a joy to own. You can knit her a birthday cake too, as well as a headband with lovely ribbon roses.

• • • • • • • • • • • • • • • • • • • • • • • • • • • • • • • • • • • • • • • • • • • • •

## YOU WILL NEED

### For Lily
Chunky: Bulky weight (CYCA #6) yarn:
100g (approximately 130 yds) in beige (A)
DK Light worsted weight (CYCA #3) yarn:
50g (approximately 154 yds) in gray (B)
Scraps of dark brown yarn for features

*Shown in:*
Bergère de France Plume, 47% polyamide,
42% acrylic, 11% wool (65 yds/60m per 50g)
2 x 50g balls in 29274 Beige
Bergère de France Norvège, 40% wool, 40%
acrylic, 20% mohair (154 yds/140m per 50g ball):
1 x 50g ball in 31126 Duvet

Needles size 7/4.5mm
Quality polyester stuffing

### For the dress
DK/Light worsted weight (CYCA #3) yarn:
50g (approximately 179 yds) in pink (C)
50g (approximately 179 yds) in white (D)

*Shown in:*
Sirdar Snuggly DK, 55% nylon, 45% acrylic
(179 yds/165m per 50g ball)
1 x 50g ball in 199 Trendy Pink
1 x 50g ball in 251 White

Needles size 6/4mm
Small length of pale pink baby ribbon

**Tip** Lily's skirt could be knitted in stockinette stitch if you prefer (see Daisy, page 123).

### For the accessories
Small amounts of cream, pale pink, deep pink and yellow DK yarn

Needles size 6/4mm
Cardboard tube 11"/27cm diameter, 2½"/6cm depth
Small piece of cardstock to make candle
Quality polyester stuffing and craft glue
9 pink ribbon roses
Piece of green and white spotted ribbon

## KNITTING NOTES

### Gauge
15 sts and 20 rows to 4"/10cm for fur and mohair yarns using size 7/4.5mm needles.
22 sts and 28 rows to 4"/10cm for DK/light worsted weight yarn using size 6/4mm needles.

### Measurements
11"/28cm tall when sitting. Circumference of belly when stuffed is about 14"/35.5cm.

### Abbreviations
See page 33.

# Lily
## Body and head
### made in one piece

Using size 7/4.5mm needles and A, cast on 20 sts.

**Next row:** Purl.

**Next row:** Inc in each st across row (40 sts).

**Next row:** Purl.

**Next row:** *K1, inc in next st; rep from * to end of (60 sts).

Cont in St st for 36 more rows.

**Decrease row (mark this row for neck of bear)**

**Next row:** *K4, skpo; rep from * to end of row (50 sts).

**Next row:** Purl.

Cont on these 50 sts for 26 more rows.

### Shape top of head

**Next row:** *K5, skpo; rep from * to last st, k1 (43 sts).

**Next and following alt rows:** Purl.

**Next RS row:** *K4, skpo; rep from * to last st, k1 (36 sts).

**Next RS row:** *K3, skpo; rep from * to last st, k1 (29 sts).

**Next RS row:** *K2, skpo; rep from * to last st, k1 (22 sts).

**Next RS row:** *K1, skpo; rep from * to last st, k1 (15 sts).

**Next RS row:** Skpo; rep to last st, k1 (8 sts).

Purl 1 row and bind off.

## Muzzle

Using size 7/4.5mm needles and B, cast on 8 sts.

**Next row:** Purl.

**Next row:** Inc 1 st at each end of row (10 sts).

**Next row:** Purl.

Repeat last 2 rows until you have 16 sts, ending with a purl row.

Work 8 rows in St st.

Dec 1 st at each end of next and following alt rows until you have 8 sts.

Work 2 rows St st and bind off.

## Ears

**make 2 in A and 2 in B**

Using size 7/4.5mm needles and A or B, cast on 10 sts.

Work in St st for 2 rows.

Inc in first and last st of every alt row to 16 sts.

Beg with a purl row, work 7 rows in St st.

**Next row:** K2tog across row (8 sts).

**Next row:** Purl.

**Next row:** K2tog across row (4 sts). Bind off.

## Arms

**make 2**

Using size 7/4.5mm needles and A, cast on 10 sts.

**Next row:** Purl.

**Next row:** *K1, inc in next st; rep from * to end of row (15 sts).

**Next row:** Purl.

**Next row:** *K1, inc in next st; rep from * to last st, k1 (22 sts).

**Next row:** Purl.

**Next row:** Inc in first and last st (24 sts).

Beg with a purl row, work 24 rows in St st.

**Next row:** *K1, skpo; rep from * to end of row (16 sts).

**Next row:** Purl.

**Next row:** K2tog across row (8 sts).

**Next row:** Purl.

**Next row:** K2tog across row (4 sts). Break yarn and run through sts left on needle. Draw up and fasten off.

## Legs

**make 2**

Using size 7/4.5mm needles and A, cast on 10 sts.

**Next row:** Purl.

**Next row:** *K1, inc in next st; rep from * to end of row (15 sts).

**Next row:** Purl.

**Next row:** *K1, inc in next st; rep from * to last st, k1 (22 sts).

**Next row:** Purl.

**Next row:** Inc in first and last st (24 sts).

**Next row:** Purl.

Repeat last 2 rows once more (26 sts).

Cont in St st for 22 rows.

### Increase for foot

**Next row:** K9, inc in each of next 8 sts, k9 (34 sts).

Beg with a purl row, work 9 rows St st.

**Next row:** K2tog across row (17 sts).

**Next row:** Purl.

**Next row:** K2tog across row to last st, k1 (9 sts).

**Next row:** Purl.

Break yarn and run through sts left on needle. Draw up and fasten off.

## Assembly

Sew the head and body seam, which runs down the back of the bear. Leave the base open to stuff.

Stuff the head first, making it nice and firm and round. Using a needle threaded with matching yarn, and beginning at the marked row for the neck, weave the yarn in and out of each stitch all the way around, beginning and ending at the seam. Pull up firmly to form the head and neck. Secure firmly at the seam. Continue to stuff the body, then close the base.

Sew the side seam of the muzzle to form a cup shape. Add some stuffing, then pin it to the front of the head, using the photos as a guide. Sew the muzzle in place. Pin the nose in the center of the muzzle with the widest part at the top. Add a bit of stuffing to pad it out slightly, then sew in place. Use the long tail of yarn left and stitch to the base of the muzzle, pulling it firmly to form the bear's mouth.

Embroider the eyes and eyebrows with dark brown yarn. Sew the ears together in pairs and attach to each side of the head.

Sew the seams on the arms, leaving the top edge open, and stuff. Attach to the shoulders of the bear on each side.

Sew the leg seams and stuff, making sure that you fill out the feet to a nice shape. Sew the legs to each side in a sitting position.

# Dress

### Front

Using size 6/4mm needles and C, cast on 73 sts.

Knit 3 rows garter stitch. Join in D.

**Begin pattern**

Begin with D and carry yarn not in use up side of work.

**Row 1:** K1, *(k2tog) twice, (yo, k1) 3 times, yo, (skpo) twice, k1; rep from * to end of row.

**Row 2:** Purl.

**Rows 3–6:** Rep rows 1 and 2 twice. Drop D and pick up C.

**Rows 7–10:** Using C, work 4 rows garter stitch.

Repeat rows 1–10 once more.

Repeat rows 1–6 once more.

**Next row:** K2tog across row to last st, k1 (37 sts).

**Next row:** Using C, knit.

**Next row (make holes for ribbon):** K2, *yo, k2tog; rep from * to last st, k1.

**Next row:** Knit.

Break C and join in D

Work 6 rows in St st.

**Shape armholes**

Bind off 3 sts at beg of next 2 rows (31 sts).

**Next row:** K1, skpo, knit to last 3 sts, k2tog, k1 (29 sts).

**Next row:** K1, purl to last st, k1. ***

Repeat the last 2 rows until you have 19 sts, ending on a purl row.

**Shape neck**

**Next row:** K1, skpo, k4, turn (leave rem sts on a stitch holder or spare needle).

**Next row:** P2tog, purl to last st, k1 (5 sts).

**Next row:** K1, skpo, k2 (4 sts).

**Next row:** P2tog, p2 (3 sts).

**Next row:** Skpo, k1 (2 sts).

**Next row:** P2tog, fasten off.

Return to sts on holder.

Slip center 5 sts onto holder for center neck, rejoin yarn to rem sts and complete to match other side, working k2tog instead of skpo.

## Back

Work as front to ***.

**Next row:** K1, skpo, k11, turn (proceed on this set of sts, leave rem sts on a holder).

**Next row:** K2, purl to last st, k1.

**Next row:** K1, skpo, knit to end (11 sts).

**Next row:** K2, purl to last st, k1.

Cont as for last 2 rows until you have 5 sts left. Leave on a stitch holder.

Rejoin yarn to rem sts, bind off 1 st, knit to last 3 sts, k2tog, k1.

Now complete to match first side, reversing shapings and working k2tog instead of skpo.

## Sleeves

### make 2

Using size 6/4mm needles and C, cast on 32 sts.

Work 3 rows in garter st.

Break C and join in D.

Change to St st and work 8 rows.

**Shape armholes**

Bind off 3 sts at beg of next 2 rows (26 sts).

**Next row:** Knit.

**Next row:** K1, purl to last st, k1.

Rep last 2 rows once more.

**Next row:** K1, skpo, knit to last 3 sts, k2tog, k1 (24 sts).

**Next row:** K1, purl to last st, k1.

Cont as for last 2 rows until you have 10 sts left.

Bind off.

## Assembly

Sew raglan seams on back, front, and sleeves. With right side of work facing, using size 6/4mm needles and D and beginning at left back, pick up and knit 5 sts from left back, 10 sts from first sleeve, 5 sts down side of neck, 5 sts from front neck, 5 sts from other side of neck, 10 sts from sleeve and 5 sts from right back (45 sts).

**Next row:** Knit.

Break D and join in C.

Knit 2 more rows in garter stitch and bind off firmly.

Embroider the heart onto the front bodice of the skirt using the duplicate-stitch method (see page 27). Mark the center stitch of the front bodice. Beginning on the first row after binding off for the armholes, center the first stitch of the heart to align with the center stitch of the body.

Now work the embroidery from the chart.

Sew sleeve and side seams on dress. Attach a small piece of ribbon on each side of the back neck and tie to fasten.

**DUPLICATE STITCH CHART (9 sts x 9 rows)**

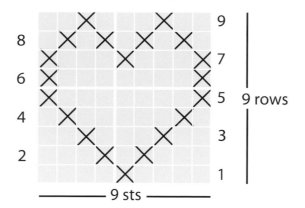

# Headband

Using size 6/4mm needles and
cream yarn, cast on 70 sts.
Knit 4 rows garter st and bind off.

## Flower

Using size 6/4mm needles and
cream yarn, cast on 50 sts.
**Next row:** Knit.
**Next row:** K2, *bind off 6 sts, k2;
rep from * to end of row (14 sts).
**Next row:** Knit the rem sts on
the needle, thus drawing in
the center of the flower.
Break yarn leaving a tail,
run the yarn through the
remaining stitches, draw up
tight and fasten off.

## Assembly

Join short ends of the headband.
Stitch the flower onto the band
to cover the join. Sew or glue
three ribbon roses to the center
of the flower.

# Birthday cake

## Side

Using size 6/4mm needles and pale pink yarn, cast on 13 sts.
Work in pattern as follows:

**Row 1:** Knit.
**Row 2:** Purl.
**Row 3:** Knit.
**Row 4:** Knit.
**Row 5:** Purl.
**Row 6:** Knit.
Repeat last 6 rows until work is long enough to stretch around cardboard tube.

## Top of cake

### worked in garter st

Using size 6/4mm needles and cream yarn, cast on 9 sts.
Knit 1 row.
Inc 1 st at each end of the next and following alt rows to 17 sts.

**Make hole for candle**

**Next row:** K8, bind off 1 st, k8.
**Next row:** Knit, cast on a stitch over the bound off stitch of previous row.
Knit 4 rows in garter stitch.
Dec 1 st at each end of next and following alt rows to 9 sts.
Bind off.

## Candle

Using size 6/4mm needles and deep pink yarn, cast on 15 sts.
Knit 10 rows St st.
Bind off.

## Flame

Using size 6/4mm needles and yellow yarn, cast on 6 sts.
Work 12 rows in St st.
Bind off.

## Assembly

Join the short ends of the side piece to form a circle. Pin the top piece of the cake inside the circle and sew in place. Slip onto the cardboard tube. Glue in place along the edges. Stuff the inside of the tube to keep the top flat.

Cut a circle of cardstock the same diameter as the tube and place the circle inside the base of the cake to cover the stuffing. Roll a piece of cardstock into a narrow cylinder approx 3"/7.5cm long to form the candle. Join the candle piece along the side edge, and slip the tube inside.

Fold the flame in half, sew the side seams, place inside the candle tube, then push into the hole made in the top of the cake. This will be a tight fit. Stitch or glue the flame in place.

With lengths of pale pink and cream yarn, make a twisted cord long enough to fit around the top of the cake. Stitch into a circle, then sew in place. Sew or glue ribbon roses onto the top of the cake. Tie ribbon around the center of the cake in a big bow.

Sunny

Sunny the panda is ready to join you for a vacation at the ocean. Wearing trendy striped beach shorts, he is just longing to ride the waves! You can even make him a surfboard to complete his outfit.

## YOU WILL NEED

### For Sunny
Aran weight (CYCA #4) yarn:
100g (approximately 174 yds) in cream (A)
100g (approximately 174 yds) in black (B)
Scraps of black DK yarn for nose

*Shown in:*
Rico Fashion Fur, 85% acrylic, 15% nylon
(87yds/80m per 50g ball):
2 x 50g balls in 001 Cream
2 x 50g balls in 005 Black

Needles size 9/5.5mm
Needles size 6/4mm
Quality polyester stuffing
1 pair of brown safety eyes

### For the shorts and surfboard
DK/Light worsted weight (CYCA #3) yarn in lime green (C), pink (D), lilac (E)
Scraps of black DK yarn for embroidery

*Shown in:*
Small amounts of Robin DK yarn in neon shades
Lime 162, Pink 146, Lilac 145

Needles size 6/4mm
Piece of plastic canvas or stiff cardstock for inner surfboard

**Tip** It isn't easy to count rows in this type of yarn so be sure to mark down the rows as you work.

## KNITTING NOTES

### Gauge
12 sts and 16 rows to 4"/10cm for fur yarn using size 9/5.5mm needles.
22 sts and 28 rows to 4"/10cm for DK yarn using size 6/4mm needles.

### Yarn notes
You may substitute the yarns listed for any eyelash or double knitting weight yarns, but be sure to check your gauge. By substituting the yarns your bear will not look quite the same as the one in the book and may be slightly smaller in size.

### Measurements
Bear: 11"/28cm tall when sitting. Circumference of belly when stuffed is about 13½"/34.5cm.
Surfboard: 9½"/24cm tall and 4¼"/11cm wide.

### Abbreviations
See page 33.

# Sunny

## Head

Using size 9/5.5mm needles and A, cast on 10 sts.

**Next row:** Purl.

**Next row:** Inc in each stitch across row (20 sts).

Beg with a purl row, work 3 rows St st.

**Next row:** *K1, inc in next st; repeat from * to end of row (30 sts).

Beg with a purl row, work 3 rows St st.

**Next row:** *K1, inc in next st; repeat from * to end of row (45 sts).

Beg with a purl row, work 11 rows St st.

### Shape top of head

**Next row:** *K1, k2tog; rep from * to end of row (30 sts).

Beg with a purl row, work 3 rows St st.

**Next row:** K2tog across row (15 sts).

**Next row:** Purl.

Break yarn and run through sts left on needle. Draw up and fasten off.

## Muzzle

Using size 9/5.5mm needles and A, cast on 8 sts.

**Next row:** Purl.

**Next row:** Inc in each st across row (16 sts).

**Next row:** Purl.

**Next row:** *K1, inc in next st; rep from * to end of row (24 sts).

**Next row:** Purl.

**Next row:** *K2, inc in next st; rep from * to end of row (32 sts).

Work 3 rows St st.

**Next row:** *K3, inc in next st; rep from * to end (40 sts).

Work in St st for 5 rows and bind off.

## Body

Using size 9/5.5mm needles and A, cast on 10 sts.

**Next row:** Purl.

**Next row:** Inc in each stitch across row (20 sts).

Beg with a purl row, work 3 rows St st.

**Next row:** *K1, inc in next st; rep from * to end of row (30 sts).

Beg with a purl row, work 3 rows St st.

**Next row:** *K1, inc in next st; rep from * to end of row (45 sts).

Beg with a purl row, cont in St st. When work measures 5"/13cm, break A and join in B.

Work in St st for a further 3"/8cm using B.

**Shape top of body**

**Next row:** *K1, k2tog; rep from * to end of row (30 sts).

Beg with a purl row, work 3 rows St st.

**Next row:** K2tog across row (15 sts).

**Next row:** Purl.

Break yarn and run through sts left on needle. Draw up and fasten off.

## Legs
make 2

Using size 9/5.5mm needles and B, cast on 8 sts.

**Next row:** Purl.

**Next row:** Inc in each st across row (16 sts).

Work 5 rows St st.

**Next row:** Inc 1 st at each end of row (18 sts).

Work 3 rows St st.

**Next row:** *K2, inc in next st; rep from * to end of row (24 sts).

Work 17 rows St st.

**Next row:** K9, inc in each of next 6 sts, k9 (30 sts).

**Next row:** Purl.

**Next row:** K12, inc in each of next 6 sts, k12 (36 sts).

Beg with a purl row, work 5 rows St st.

**Next row:** K2tog across row (18 sts).

**Next row:** Purl.

**Next row:** K2tog across row (9 sts).

**Next row:** Purl.

Break yarn and run through sts left on needle. Draw up and fasten off.

## Arms

**make 2**

Using size 9/5.5mm needles and B, cast on 8 sts.

**Next row:** Purl.

**Next row:** Inc in each st across row (16 sts).

**Next row:** Purl.

Work 4 rows St st.

**Next row:** Inc 1 st at each end (18 sts).

Work 13 rows St st.

**Next row:** *K2, inc in next st; rep from * to end of row (24 sts).

Work 7 rows St st.

**Next row:** K2tog across row (12 sts).

**Next row:** Purl.

**Next row:** K2tog across row (6 sts).

**Next row:** Purl.

Break yarn and run through sts left on needle. Draw up and fasten off.

## Ears

**make 2**

Using size 9/5.5mm needles and B, cast on 8 sts.

**Next row:** Purl.

**Next row:** Inc in each st across row (16 sts).

Work 5 rows St st.

**Next row:** K2tog across row (8 sts).

**Next row:** Purl.

**Next row:** K2tog across row (4 sts).

Bind off.

## Eye patches

**make 2**

Using size 9/5.5mm needles and B, cast on 6 sts.

**Next row:** Purl.

**Next row:** Inc 1 st at each end of row (8 sts).

**Next row:** Purl.

Work 6 rows in St st.

**Next row:** Dec 1 st at each end of next and following alt rows until you have 2 sts.

**Next row:** Purl.

Bind off.

## Nose

Using size 6/4mm needles and black yarn, cast on 10 sts.

Work 12 rows in garter stitch.

**Next row:** K2tog at each end of row (8 sts).

**Next row:** Knit.

Repeat last 2 rows until you have 2 sts.

Bind off.

## Assembly

The seams run down the back of the head and body, and the undersides of the arms and legs. Sew the body seam first, leaving the cast-on end open for stuffing. Stuff firmly to a nice rounded shape. Close the opening.

Sew the head in the same way, leaving an opening at the base for stuffing. Stuff partially, as the eyes still have to be inserted, and do not close the base yet.

Sew the seams on the arms, leaving the cast-on edge open for stuffing. To stuff the arms, push plenty of stuffing down into the paw first then continue stuffing the rest of the arm. Sew the leg seams. Push extra stuffing into the feet to shape.

Sew the muzzle seam down the bottom of muzzle. Pin to the front of the bear's head and add stuffing to shape. It may take a little time to make this look right. Sew the muzzle onto the face, adding more stuffing to shape. Sew the nose to the center of the muzzle.

Pin the ears onto the head on each side, making them level. With some matching yarn, curl the ears into a semi-circular shape, then stitch in place.

Sew the eye patches to each side of the bear's head. Push safety eyes through the eye patches, positioning them correctly before snapping on the backs. Embroider the mouth with black yarn.

Pin the legs in place in a sitting position, making them level. Sew the legs in place.

Pin the arms in position and sew firmly in place. Finally, sew the bear's head onto the body.

# Shorts

**make 2**

Using size 6/4mm needles and C, cast on 40 sts.

Work in k2, p2 rib for 4 rows.

**Next row (eyelet holes for cord):**

*K2, yo, p2tog; rep from * to end of row.

Work 3 more rows in k2, p2 rib.

Change to D and work 10 rows St st.

Change to E and work 4 rows St st.

**Next row:** K19, m1, k2, m1, k19 (42 sts).

**Next row:** Purl.

**Next row:** K20, m1, k2, m1, k20 (44 sts).

**Next row:** Purl.

**Divide for legs**

**Next row:** K21, bind off 2 sts, k21. Proceed on first set of sts as follows:

**Next row:** Purl.

Work 5 rows St st.

Change to garter stitch and work 5 rows. Bind off.

Rejoin yarn to remaining sts and complete to match first leg.

## Stripe

Using size 6/4mm needles and black yarn, cast on 36 sts. Work 6 rows garter stitch and bind off.

## Assembly

Sew the side seams and leg seams. Using lime yarn, make a twisted cord and thread it through the waist. Sew the stripe onto the shorts.

# Surfboard

### make 2

Using size 6/4mm needles and C, cast on 13 sts, join in E and cast on 13 sts (26 sts).

Work in St st for 7½"/19cm, being sure to twist the yarns together when changing colors to prevent holes from forming in the fabric. Cont in E only (cont in C only when working the other side).

Work 2 rows St st.

K2tog at each end of next and following alt rows to 14 sts. Bind off.

## Wristband

Using size 6/4mm needles and lilac yarn, cast on 8 sts.

Knit 34 rows in garter st and bind off.

## Assembly

Cut some stiff cardstock or plastic canvas to measure 9½"/24cm long and 4¼"/11cm wide. Round the corners off at one end for the top of the surfboard.

Sew the seam around the two knitted pieces, then turn right sides out. Slip in the shaped cardstock or plastic canvas and stretch a little for a snug fit. Sew the base closed neatly. You can embroider a couple of vertical lines using black yarn or a number onto one side if you like.

For the wrist band, sew the short ends together. Make a twisted cord in lilac and attach to the wristband. Attach the cord and band to the top of the surfboard.

Mortimer

Make this earnest bear as a keepsake for a special graduate. You can personalize the colors to appeal to the recipient, perhaps matching their college colors. You could even add initials onto the gown with some simple embroidery.

## YOU WILL NEED

### For Mortimer

Aran weight (CYCA #4) yarn:
100g (approximately 174 yds) dark brown
50g (approximately 87 yds) medium brown
Scraps of black DK yarn for nose and features

*Shown in:*
Rico Fashion Fur, 85% acrylic, 15% nylon
(87 yds/80m per 50g ball):
2 x 50g balls 003 Brown (A)
1 x 50g ball medium brown (B)

Needles size 9/5.5mm
Needles size 6/4mm
Quality polyester stuffing
1 pair of safety eyes

### For the gown and accessories

DK/Light worsted weight (CYCA #3) yarn:
100g (approximately 358 yds) blue
50g (approximately 179 yds) gold
Small amount of white (E)

*Shown in:*
Sirdar Snuggly DK, 55% nylon, 45% acrylic
(179 yds/164m per 50g):
2 x 50g ball Royal Blue (C)
1 x 50g ball Gold (D)

Needles size 6/4mm
Length of red satin ribbon
4"/10cm square of stiff cardstock or plastic canvas

### KNITTING NOTES

### Gauge

12 sts and 16 rows to 4"/10cm for fur yarn using size 9/5.5mm needles.
22 sts and 28 rows to 4"/10cm for DK yarn using size 6/4mm needles.

### Yarn notes

You may substitute the yarns listed for any eyelash or double knitting weight yarns, but be sure to check your gauge. By substituting the yarns your bear will not look quite the same as the one in the book.

### Measurements

11"/28cm tall when sitting.
Circumference of belly when stuffed is about 13½"/34.5cm.

### Abbreviations

See page 33.

> **Tip** It isn't easy to count rows in this type of yarn so be sure to mark down the rows as you work.

# Mortimer

## Head

Using size 9/5.5mm needles and A, cast on 10 sts.

**Next row:** Purl.

**Next row:** Inc in each stitch across row (20 sts).

Beg with a purl row, work 3 rows St st.

**Next row:** *K1, inc in next st; repeat from * to end of row (30 sts).

Beg with a purl row, work 3 rows St st.

**Next row:** *K1, inc in next st; repeat from * to end of row (45 sts).

Beg with a purl row, work 11 rows St st.

**Shape top of head**

**Next row:** *K1, k2tog; rep from * to end of row (30 sts).

Beg with a purl row, work 3 rows St st.

**Next row:** K2tog across row (15 sts).

**Next row:** Purl.

Break yarn and run through sts left on needle. Draw up and fasten off.

## Muzzle

Using size 6/4mm needles and B, cast on 8 sts.

**Next row:** Purl.

**Next row:** Inc in each st across row (16 sts).

**Next row:** Purl.

**Next row:** *K1, inc in next st; rep from * to end of row (24 sts).

**Next row:** Purl.

Work 4 rows St st.

**Next row:** *K1, inc in next st; rep from * to end of row (36 sts).

Work in St st for 6 rows and bind off.

## Nose

Using size 6/4mm needles and black yarn, cast on 8 sts.

Work 4 rows in St st.

**Next row:** K2tog, work to last 2 sts, k2tog (6 sts).

**Next row:** Purl.

**Next row:** K2tog, k2, k2tog (4 sts).

**Next row:** Purl.

**Next row:** K2tog twice (2 sts).

**Next row:** Purl.

**Next row:** K2tog and fasten off. Leave a long tail of yarn to form the mouth.

## Body

Using size 9/5.5mm needles and A, cast on 10 sts.

**Next row:** Purl.

**Next row:** Inc in each st across row (20 sts).

Beg with a purl row, work 3 rows St st.

**Next row:** *K1, inc in next st; rep from * to end of row (30 sts).

Beg with a purl row, work 3 rows St st.

**Next row:** *K1, inc in next st; rep from * to end of row (45 sts).

Beg with a purl row, work 31 rows St st.

### Shape top of body

**Next row:** *K1, k2tog; rep from * to end of row (30 sts).

Beg with a purl row, work 3 rows St st.

**Next row:** K2tog across row (15 sts).

**Next row:** Purl.

Break yarn and run through sts left on needle. Draw up and fasten off.

## Legs
### make 2

Using size 9/5.5mm needles and A, cast on 8 sts.

**Next row:** Purl.

**Next row:** Inc in each st across row (16 sts).

Work in St st for 5 rows.

**Next row:** Inc 1 st at each end of row (18 sts).

Work 3 rows St st.

**Next row:** *K2, inc in next st; rep from * to end of row (24 sts).

Work 11 rows St st.

**Next row:** *K1, k2tog; rep from * to end of row (16 sts).

Work 7 rows St st.

**Next row:** K5, inc in each of next 6 sts, k5 (22 sts).

**Next row:** Purl.

**Next row:** K5, (k1, inc1) 6 times, k5 (28 sts).

Work 5 rows St st and bind off loosely.

### Arms
**make 2**

Using size 9/5.5mm needles and A, cast on 8 sts.

**Next row:** Purl.

**Next row:** Inc in each st across row (16 sts).

**Next row:** Purl.

Work 4 rows St st.

**Next row:** Inc 1 st at each end of row (18 sts).

Work 13 rows St st.

**Next row:** *K2, inc in next st; rep from * to end of row (24 sts).

Work 7 rows St st.

**Next row:** K2tog across row (12 sts).

**Next row:** Purl.

**Next row:** K2tog across row (6 sts). Bind off.

### Feet pads
**make 2**

Using size 6/4mm needles and B, cast on 8 sts.

**Next row:** Purl.

Inc 1 st at each end of next and following alt rows until you have 14 sts.

Knit 11 rows in St st.

Dec 1 st at each end of next and following alt rows until you have 8 sts.

Bind off.

### Ears
**make 2**

Using size 9/5.5mm needles and A, cast on 8 sts.

**Next row:** Purl.

**Next row:** Inc in each st across row (16 sts).

Work 5 rows St st.

**Next row:** K2tog across row (8 sts).

**Next row:** Purl.

**Next row:** K2tog across row (4 sts). Bind off.

## Assembly

Sewing with this type of yarn is challenging. Use a big-eyed, blunt-ended needle and short lengths of yarn. Seams will run down the back of the head and body, and the undersides of the arms and legs.

Sew the body seam first, leaving one end open to stuff. Stuff firmly to a nice rounded shape, then close the opening. Sew the head the same way, leaving an opening to stuff. Only partially stuff the head because you need to insert the safety eyes before closing the opening. Sew the muzzle seam, which is underneath. Pin the muzzle to the front of the head and add stuffing to shape. Sew the muzzle onto the face, adding more stuffing for a good shape. Sew the nose in place. Insert the safety eyes on each side of the nose and click into place. Finish stuffing the head and close the opening.

Pin the ears onto the head on each side, making them level. With matching yarn, curl the ears into a semicircular shape and stitch in place on the head. Sew the arm seams, leavng the cast-on edge open for stuffing. To stuff the arms, push plenty of stuffing down into the paw, then continue stuffing the rest of the arm.

Sew the leg seams and stuff them, leaving the base open so you can sew on the foot pads. Pin a foot pad in place around the foot opening, adding more stuffing if needed. Carefully sew the pads in place around the opening.

Pin the legs to the bear in a sitting position. Sew them in place, making them level. Pin and sew the arms in position. Sew the bear's head onto the body.

# Gown

Using size 6/4mm needles and C, cast on 50 sts.

Work 4 rows in garter stitch.

**Next row:** Knit.

**Next row:** K4, purl to last 4 sts, k4.

Repeat the last 2 rows 18 times more.

Work 6 rows garter stitch.

**Divide for fronts**

**Next row:** K20, place sts on holder, bind off 10 sts, k20.

**First side**

**Next row:** K2tog, knit to end of row (19 sts).

**Next row:** K4, purl to last 2 sts, k2.

**Next row:** K2, k2tog, knit to end (18 sts).

**Next row:** K4, purl to last 2 sts, k2.

Repeat last 2 rows once more (17 sts).

Work until front matches back, ending on a purl row.

Work 4 rows garter stitch.

Bind off.

Place remaining stitches on needle, rejoin yarn, and complete to match first side, reversing the shaping.

## Sash

**make 2**

Using size 6/4mm needles and C, cast on 50 sts.

Knit 2 rows garter stitch.

Join in D and, beginning with a purl row, dec 1 st at each end of every row for next 5 rows. Break D.

Join in C. Work 3 rows garter stitch, still decreasing at each end of every row.

Bind off.

## Assembly

Fold the gown in half at the shoulders and join the side seams for approx 1¼"/3cm. Join the short ends of the sash, matching the colors. You should have a neat point in the center of the back and front. Fold the sash in half, matching points to points. Pin one point to the center back of the gown, then pin the sash on each side of the shoulders. Fold the sash over both fronts. Tack down each side but leave the point free. Slip the gown onto the bear and arrange the sash to lay flat on each side.

# Mortarboard

## Top

Using size 6/4mm needles and C,
cast on 24 sts.
Work in St st for 8"/20cm. Bind off.

## Base

Using size 6/4mm needles and C,
cast on 11 sts.
Work in garter stitch for 8"/20cm.
Bind off.

## Assembly

Fold the top of the mortarboard
piece in half, then join the two short
side seams. Insert a square of stiff
cardstock or plastic canvas. Sew up
the remaining edge.

Fold the base in half lengthways.
Sew the seam. Join into a circle and
sew the short ends together. Sew
the circle centrally to one side of
the top.

Using C, make a twisted chain
and tassel (see page 31) and sew to
the center top of the mortarboard.

# Diploma

Using size 6/4mm needles and E,
cast on 26 sts.
Knit 4 rows garter stitch.
**Next row:** K2, purl to last 2 sts, k2.
**Next row:** Knit.
Repeat last 2 rows 11 times more.
Work 4 rows garter stitch and
bind off.

## Assembly

Roll the scroll into a cylinder
and sew the sides. Tie a piece
of red ribbon around the
center of the scroll.

# Mr. Tubbs

Mr. Tubbs is just waiting to be hugged. His faded tweedy look and endearing face will soon melt your heart. He wears a waistcoat to keep out the chills on cooler days. He is a very easy-to-knit bear, using just reverse stockinette stitch and garter stitch.

## YOU WILL NEED

### For Mr. Tubbs

DK/Light worsted weight (CYCA #3) yarn:
100g (approximately 262 yds) in brown (A)
100g (approximately 326 yds) in green (B)
Scraps of black DK yarn for nose and
embroidered features

*Shown in:*
James C Brett Marble DK, 100% acrylic
(262 yds/240m per 100g ball):
1 x 100g ball in MT8 Autumn
Stylecraft Life DK, 75% acrylic, 25% wool
(326 yds/298m per 100g ball):
1 x 100g ball in 2318 Bracken

Needles size 7/4.5mm
Needles size 6/4mm
Quality polyester stuffing

### For the waistcoat

DK/Light worsted weight (CYCA #3) yarn:
100g (approximately 326 yds) in orange (C)

*Shown in:*
Stylecraft Life DK, 75% acrylic, 25% wool
(326 yds/298m per 100g ball):
1 x 100g ball in 2312 Copper

Needles size 7/4.5mm

## KNITTING NOTES

### Gauge

20 sts and 26 rows to 4"/10cm using
size 7/4.5mm needles.

### Yarn notes

Any DK weight yarn will work with this project.
Check your gauge beforehand and change
needle size if necessary.

### Measurements

11"/28cm tall when sitting. Circumference of belly
when stuffed is about 14"/35.5cm.

### Abbreviations

See page 33.

# Mr. Tubbs

## Body and head

### made in one piece

Using size 7/4.5mm needles and A, cast on 20 sts.

**Next row:** Purl.

**Next row:** Inc in each st across row (40 sts).

**Next row:** Purl.

**Next row:** *K1, inc in next st; rep from * to end of row (60 sts).

Cont even in St st for 39 more rows.

**Decrease row (mark this row for neck of bear)**

**Next row:** *K4, skpo; rep from * to end of row (50 sts).

**Next row:** Purl.

Cont in St st on these 50 sts for 24 more rows.

## Shape top of head

**Next row:** *K5, skpo; rep from * to last st, k1 (43 sts).

**Next and following alt rows:** Purl.

**Next WS row:** *K4, skpo; rep from * to last st, k1 (36 sts).

**Next WS row:** *K3, skpo; rep from * to last st, k1 (29 sts).

**Next WS row:** *K2, skpo; rep from * to last st, k1 (22 sts).

**Next WS row:** *K1, skpo; rep from * to last st, k1 (15 sts).

**Next WS row:** Skpo; rep to last st, k1 (8 sts).

Purl 1 row and bind off.

## Muzzle

Using size 6/4mm needles and B, cast on 10 sts.

**Next row:** Purl.

**Next row:** Inc in each st across row (20 sts).

**Next row:** Purl.

**Next row:** *K1, inc in next st; rep from * to end of row (30 sts).

**Next row:** Purl.

**Next row:** *K2, inc in next st; rep from * to end of row (40 sts).

**Next row:** Purl.

**Next row:** *K3, inc in next st; rep from * to end of row (50 sts).

**Next row:** Purl.

**Next row:** *K4, inc in next st; rep from * to end of row (60 sts).

**Next row:** Purl.

Work 4 rows in St st and bind off.

## Ears
### make 2 in A and 2 in B
Using size 6/4mm needles and A,
cast on 10 sts.

Work in St st for 2 rows.

**Next row:** Inc 1 st at each end of
every alt row to 16 sts.

Beg with a purl row, work 5 rows
work in St st.

**Next row:** K2tog across row (8 sts).

**Next row:** Purl.

**Next row:** K2tog across row.
Bind off.

## Right arm
Using size 7/4.5mm needles and A,
cast on 10 sts.

**Next row:** Purl.

**Next row:** *K1, inc in next st; rep
from * to end of row (15 sts).

**Next row:** Purl.

**Next row:** *K1, inc in next st; rep
from * to last st, k1 (22 sts).

**Next row:** Purl.

**Next row:** Inc in first and last st
(24 sts).

Beg with a purl row, work 17 rows
in St st.

### Shape arm
**Next row:** K12, turn and purl back.

**Next row:** K13, turn and purl back.

**Next row:** K14, turn and purl back.

**Next row:** K15, turn and purl back.

**Next row:** Knit across all sts.

**Next row:** Purl.

Work 8 rows in st st.

**Next row:** *K1, skpo; rep from * to
end of row (16 sts).

**Next row:** Purl.

**Next row:** K2tog across row (8 sts).

**Next row:** Purl.

**Next row:** K2tog across row (4 sts).
Break yarn and run through sts left
on needle. Draw up and fasten off.

## Left arm

Using size 7/4.5mm needles and A, cast on 10 sts.

**Next row:** Purl.

**Next row:** *K1, inc in next st; rep from * to end of row (15 sts).

**Next row:** Purl.

**Next row:** *K1, inc in next st; rep from * to last st, k1 (22 sts).

**Next row:** Purl.

**Next row:** Inc in first and last st (24 sts).

Beg with a purl row, work 18 rows in St st.

### Shape arm

**Next row:** P12, turn and knit back.

**Next row:** P13, turn and knit back.

**Next row:** P14, turn and knit back.

**Next row:** P15, turn and knit back.

**Next row:** Purl across all sts.

Work 8 rows in St st.

**Next row:** *K1, skpo; rep from * to end of row (16 sts).

**Next row:** Purl.

**Next row:** K2tog across row (8 sts).

**Next row:** Purl.

**Next row:** K2tog across row (4 sts).

Break yarn and run through sts left on needle. Draw up and fasten off.

## Legs

### make 2

Using size 7/4.5mm needles and A, cast on 10 sts.

**Next row:** Purl.

**Next row:** *K1, inc in next st; rep from * across row (15 sts).

**Next row:** Purl.

**Next row:** *K1, inc in next st; rep from * to last st, k1 (22 sts).

**Next row:** Purl.

**Next row:** Inc in first and last st (24 sts).

**Next row:** Purl.

Repeat last 2 rows once more (26 sts).

Cont in St st for 20 rows.

### Increase for foot

**Next row:** K9, inc in each of next 8 sts, k9 (34 sts).

Beg with a purl row, work 9 rows in St st.

**Next row:** K2tog across row (17 sts).

**Next row:** Purl.

**Next row:** K2tog across row to last st, k1 (9 sts).

**Next row:** Purl.

Break yarn and run through sts left on needle. Draw up and fasten off.

## Nose

Using size 6/4mm needles and black yarn, cast on 8 sts.

Work 4 rows in St st.

**Next row:** K2tog, work to last 2 sts, k2tog (6 sts).

**Next row:** Purl.

**Next row:** K2tog, k2, k2tog (4 sts).

**Next row:** Purl.

**Next row:** K2tog twice.

**Next row:** Purl.

**Next row:** K2tog and fasten off.

Leave a long tail of yarn to form the mouth.

## Assembly

NOTE: The purl side of the St st is the right side of the fabric, *except* for the muzzle and inner ears, which are smooth St st.

Begin with the head and body of the bear. Sew the back seam, which runs down the back of the bear, leaving the base open to stuff. Stuff the head first, making it nice and firm and round. With a needle threaded with matching yarn, begin at the marked row for the neck and weave the yarn in and out of every stitch all the way around, starting and ending at the seam. Pull up firmly to form the head and neck. Secure well at the seam. Continue to stuff the body, then close the base.

Sew the side seam of the muzzle to form a cup shape. Add some stuffing, then pin it to the front of the bear, using the photos as a guide. Sew the muzzle in place. Pin the nose in the center of the muzzle with the widest part at the top. Add a tiny bit of stuffing to pad it

out slightly, then sew in place. Use the long tail of yarn left and stitch to the base of the muzzle, pulling it firmly to form the bear's mouth. Embroider the eyes and eyebrows using black yarn.

Sew the ears together in pairs, with the dark brown ears inside the tweed ears. Attach to each side of the head.

Sew the seams on the arms, leaving the top edge open, and stuff. Attach to the shoulders of the bear on each side. Sew the leg seams and stuff, making sure that you fill out the feet for a nice shape. Sew the legs to each side in a sitting position.

# Waistcoat

### Back

Using size 7/4.5mm needles and C, cast on 43 sts.

Work 6 rows in garter stitch.

**Begin pattern**

Work 4 rows St st.

Work 2 rows in seed stitch.

These 6 rows form the pattern.

Repeat last 6 rows once more.

Work 2 rows in St st.

**Shape armhole, keeping in pattern as set**

Bind off 4 sts at beg of next 2 rows.

Dec 1 st at each end of next and following alt rows to 29 sts.

Cont in pattern until you have worked 32 patterned rows in total.

Bind off.

### Right front

Using size 7/4.5mm needles and C, cast on 23 sts.

Work 6 rows garter stitch.

**Begin pattern**

Work 4 rows in St st.

Work 2 rows in seed stitch.

Repeat last 6 rows once more. **

Work 1 row St st, ending with WS facing for next row.

**Shape armhole and neck, keeping in pattern as set**

**Next row:** Bind off 4 sts, purl to end of row.

Dec 1 st at armhole edge on next and following 3 alt rows and *at the same time* dec 1 st at front edge on every row until you have 7 sts.

Cont in pattern until front matches back to shoulders.

Bind off.

### Left front

Work as right front to **.

Work 2 rows in St st, ending with RS facing for next row.

**Shape armhole and neck, keeping in pattern as set**

**Next row:** Bind off 4 sts, knit to end of row.

**Next row:** Purl.

Dec 1 st at armhole edge on next and following 3 alt rows and *at the same time* dec 1 st at front edge on every row until you have 7 sts.

Cont in pattern until front matches back to shoulders.

Bind off.

## Button loops

**make 2**

Using size 7/4.5mm needles and C, cast on 12 sts.
Bind off.

## Assembly

Sew the side seams of the waistcoat and join the shoulder seams. Sew on the buttons and button loops, overlapping the fronts slightly. Slip on to the bear.

## Buttons

**make 2**

Using size 7/4.5mm needles and C, cast on 3 sts.

**Next row:** Purl.

**Next row:** Inc in each st across row (6 sts).

**Next row:** Purl.

**Next row:** Inc in each st across row (12 sts).

**Next row:** Purl.

Break yarn and run through sts on needle, draw up tight and fasten off. Join the side seam and form into a tight ball, flattening slightly to form the button shape; secure with a few stitches at base.

Trixie

This bear is armed and ready for shopping the big sales! Complete with her own purse, she will soon become a much loved companion for any youngster. Novice knitters can knit the sweater in a single color instead of using the panda motif if it proves too challenging.

## YOU WILL NEED

### For Trixie

Aran weight (CYCA #4) yarn:
100g (approximately 174 yds) in dark brown
DK/Light worsted (CYCA #3) yarn:
50g (approximately 87 yds) in medium brown
Scraps of black yarn for nose and features

*Shown in:*
Rico Fashion Fur, 85% acrylic, 15% nylon
(87 yds/80m per 50g ball):
2 x 50g balls Dark Brown (A)
1 x 50g ball mid-brown DK yarn (B)

Needles size 9/5.5mm
Needles size 6/4mm
Quality polyester stuffing
1 pair of safety eyes

### For the outfit

Light worsted weight (CYCA #3) yarn:
50g (approximately 179 yds) in pink
50g (approximately 179 yds) in cream
50g (approximately 179 yds) in light green
Scraps of black fashion fur or eyelash yarn

*Shown in:*
Sirdar Snuggly DK, 55% nylon, 45% acrylic
(179 yds/165m per 50g)
1 x 50g ball in 443 Pink Plum (C)
1 x 50g ball in 303 Cream (D)
1 x 50g ball in 188 Peaceful (E)

Needles size 6/4mm
Black embroidery thread
Small ribbon bow

### For the shoes and purse

Scraps of DK left over from outfit
Needles size 6/4mm
Teddy bear sew-on patch for purse
Ribbon to close purse

## KNITTING NOTES

### Gauge

12 sts and 16 rows to 4"/10cm for fur yarn using size 9/5.5mm needles.
22 sts and 28 rows to 4"/10cm for DK yarn using size 6/4mm needles.

### Yarn notes

You may substitute the yarns listed for any eyelash or double knitting weight yarns, but check your gauge. By substituting the yarns your bear will not look quite the same as the one in the book and therefore may be slightly smaller in size.

### Measurements

11"/28cm tall when sitting. Circumference of belly when stuffed is about 14"/35.5cm.

### Abbreviations

See page 33.

**Tip** It isn't easy to count rows in this type of yarn so be sure to mark down the rows as you work.

# Trixie

## Head

Using size 9/5.5mm needles and A, cast on 10 sts.

**Next row:** Purl.

**Next row:** Inc in each stitch across row (20 sts).

Beg with a purl row, work 3 rows St st.

**Next row:** *K1, inc in next st; rep from * to end of row (30 sts).

Beg with a purl row, work 3 rows St st.

**Next row:** *K1, inc in next st; rep from * to end of row (45 sts).

Beg with a purl row, work 11 rows St st.

### Shape top of head

**Next row:** *K1, k2tog; rep from * to end of row (30 sts).

Beg with a purl row, work 3 rows St st.

**Next row:** K2tog all across row (15 sts).

**Next row:** Purl.

**Next row:** K2tog across row to last st, k1.

Break yarn and run through sts left on needle. Draw up and fasten off.

## Muzzle

Using size 6/4mm needles and B, cast on 8 sts.

**Next row:** Purl.

**Next row:** Inc in each stitch across row (16 sts).

**Next row:** Purl.

**Next row:** *K1, inc in next st; rep from * to end of row (24 sts).

**Next row:** Purl.

**Next row:** *K2, inc in next st; rep from * to end of row (32 sts).

Work 3 rows St st.

**Next row:** *K3, inc in next st; rep from * to end of row (40 sts).

Work in St st for 5 rows and bind off.

## Nose

Using size 6/4mm needles and black yarn, cast on 8 sts.

Work 4 rows St st.

**Next row:** K2tog, work to last 2 sts, k2tog (6 sts).

**Next row:** Purl.

**Next row:** K2tog, k2, k2tog (4 sts).

**Next row:** Purl.

**Next row:** K2tog twice (2 sts).

**Next row:** Purl.

**Next row:** K2tog and fasten off. Leave a long tail of yarn to form the mouth.

## Body

Using size 9/5.5mm needles and A, cast on 10 sts.

**Next row:** Purl.

**Next row:** Inc in each stitch across row (20 sts).

Beg with a purl row, work 3 rows St st.

**Next row:** *K1, inc in next st; rep from * to end of row (30 sts).

Beg with a purl row, work 3 rows St st.

**Next row:** *K1, inc in next st; rep from * to end of row (45 sts).

Beg with a purl row, work 31 rows St st.

**Shape top of body**

**Next row:** *K1, k2tog; rep from * to end of row (30 sts).

Beg with a purl row, work 3 rows St st.

**Next row:** K2tog across row (15 sts).

**Next row:** Purl.

Break yarn and run through sts left on needle. Draw up and fasten off.

## Legs
### make 2

Using size 9/5.5mm needles and A, cast on 8 sts.

**Next row:** Purl.

**Next row:** Inc in each st across row (16 sts).

Work in St st for 5 rows.

**Next row:** Inc 1 st at each end of row (18 sts).

Work 3 rows St st.

**Next row:** *K2, inc in next st; rep from * to end of row (24 sts).

Work 17 rows St st.

**Next row:** K9, inc in each of next 6 sts, k9 (30 sts).

**Next row:** Purl.

**Next row:** K12, inc in each of next 6 sts, k12 (36 sts).

Beg with a purl row, work 5 rows St st.

**Next row:** K2tog across row (18 sts).

**Next row:** Purl.

**Next row:** K2tog across row (9 sts).

**Next row:** Purl.

Break yarn and run through sts left on needle. Draw up and fasten off.

## Arms
### make 2

Using size 9/5.5mm needles and A, cast on 8 sts.

**Next row:** Purl.

**Next row:** Inc in each st across row (16 sts).

**Next row:** Purl.

Work 4 rows St st.

**Next row:** Inc 1 st at each end (18 sts).

Work 13 rows St st.

**Next row:** *K2, inc in next st; rep from * to end of row (24 sts).

Work 7 rows St st.

**Next row:** K2tog across row (12 sts).

**Next row:** Purl.

**Next row:** K2tog across row (6 sts).

**Next row:** Purl.

Break yarn and run through sts left on needle. Draw up and fasten off.

### Outer ears

**make 2**

Using size 9/5.5mm needles and A, cast on 8 sts.

**Next row:** Purl.

**Next row:** Inc in each st across row (16 sts).

Work 5 rows St st.

**Next row:** K2tog across row (8 sts).

**Next row:** Purl.

**Next row:** K2tog across row (4 sts). Bind off.

### Inner ears

**make 2**

Using size 6/4mm needles and B, cast on 10 sts.

**Next row:** Purl.

**Next row:** Inc in each st across row (20 sts).

Work 5 rows St st.

**Next row:** K2tog across row (10 sts).

**Next row:** Purl.

**Next row:** K2tog across row (5 sts).

**Next row:** Purl.

Bind off.

### Assembly

Sewing up with this type of yarn can be challenging. Use a big-eyed, blunt-ended needle and short lengths of yarn. Seams will run down the back of the head and body, and the undersides of the arms and legs.

Sew the body seam first, leaving the cast-on end open to stuff. Stuff firmly to a nice rounded shape. Close the gap. Sew the head in the same way, leaving an opening to stuff. Partially stuff the head as you need to insert safety eyes before closing.

Sew the muzzle seam, which will run underneath. Pin the muzzle to the front of the bear's head and add stuffing to shape. Sew it onto the face, adding more stuffing to make a good shape. Sew the nose in place. Insert the eyes on each side of the nose, and click into place. Finish stuffing the head and close the gap.

Stitch the inner and outer ears together. With some matching yarn, curl the ears into a semicircular shape and stitch in place onto the head.

Sew the seams on the arms, leaving the cast-on edge open for stuffing. To stuff the arms, push plenty of stuffing down into the paw first then continue stuffing the rest of the arm. Sew the leg seams and stuff as for arms.

Pin on the legs in a sitting position, making them level. Sew in place. Pin the arms in position as you did with the legs and sew firmly in place. Finally, sew the bear's head onto the body.

# Outfit

## Back of top

Using size 6/4mm needles and C, cast on 38 sts.
Work in k2, p2 rib for 4 rows.
Change to St st and work 32 rows.
Change to k2, p2 rib and work 4 rows.
Bind off.

## Front of top

Work as for back until you have completed 8 rows St st.
Work panda's head from chart, reading rows from right to left on RS rows and from left to right on WS rows. You will need to join in separate small balls of C on each side of D, twisting the yarns together on the wrong sides as you do to prevent holes in your work.

**Row 1:** K17C , k4D, k17C.
Continue until you have worked all 12 rows. Break D and continue in C only.
Complete to match back. Bind off.

## Sleeves
### make 2

Using size 6/4mm needles and C, cast on 28 sts.
Work 4 rows in k2, p2 rib. Join in E and D and work in St st in a stripe sequence of 2 rows D, 2 rows E, 2 rows C.
Work 18 rows in St st stripe patt.
Bind off.

## PANDA HEAD CHART (12 sts x 12 rows)

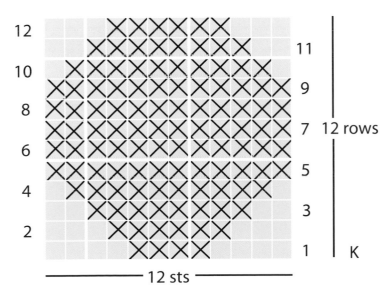

## Assembly

Sew shoulder seams on back and front for approximately ¾"/2cm. Sew the sleeves to back and front on each side. Sew the side and sleeve seams.

## Panda features

Using size 6/4mm needles and some black fashion fur yarn, cast on 4 sts. Knit two rows and bind off. Make another piece the same. Sew ears to each side of the head. Using fashion fur, embroider the eyes. Embroider the nose and mouth with black embroidery floss. Sew ribbon bow to top of head.

## Pants

**make 2**

Using size 6/4mm needles and C, cast on 40 sts.

Work in k2, p2 rib for 4 rows.

**Next row (make holes for cord):**

*K2, yo, p2tog; rep from * to end of row.

Work 3 more rows in k2, p2 rib.

Join in E and D and work St st in a stripe sequence of 2 rows D, 2 rows E, 2 rows C.

Work 16 rows in striped St st. Keeping stripe pattern as set throughout, proceed as follows:

**Next row:** K19, m1, k2, m1, k19 (42 sts).

**Next row:** Purl.

**Next row:** K20, m1, k2, m1, k20 (44 sts).

**Next row:** Purl.

**Divide for legs**

**Next row:** K21, bind off 2 sts, k21.

Proceed on first 21 sts as follows:

**Next row:** Purl.

Cont on this set of sts and work in St st stripe sequence until you have completed 34 rows in total, decreasing 1 st in the center of the last row.

Break D and E and cont in C only.

Change to k2, p2 rib and work 4 rows. Bind off in rib.

Work other side to match.

## Assembly

Sew the side seams and leg seams. Using C, make a twisted cord and thread through waist.

# Bow

Using size 6/4mm needles and C, cast on 30 sts.

Work 2 rows in garter stitch.

Join D and work 2 rows garter stitch.

Join E and work 2 rows garter stitch.

Join C and work 2 rows garter stitch.

Bind off.

## Assembly

Join the short ends. Fold the work in half with the join at center back. Run a gathering thread of C through the center of the piece. Draw up firmly to form bow shape. Stitch to bear's head.

## Shoes

**make 2**

Using size 6/4mm needles and E, cast on 30 sts.

**Next row:** Knit.

**Next row:** Inc in first and last st (32 sts).

**Next row:** Knit.

**Next row:** Inc in first and last st (34 sts).

Knit 2 rows.

**Next row:** K12, inc in each of next 10 sts, k12 (44 sts).

Knit 10 rows.

**Next row:** K12, (k2tog) 10 times, k12 (34 sts).

Knit 2 rows. Join in C.

Knit 1 row in C, and bind off.

## Assembly

Join sole and back seam. Make a tiny pompom (see page 79) and sew to the front of the shoe.

## Purse

### Front

Using size 6/4mm needles and E, cast on 16 sts.

Knit 2 rows.

Inc at each end of next and following alt rows to 20 sts.

**Next row:** Knit.

**Next row:** K7, p6, k7.

Repeat last 2 rows 11 times more.

Dec 1 st at each end of next and following alt rows to 10 sts.

Knit 2 rows.

Inc 1 st at each end of every row to 16 sts.

Knit 4 rows and bind off.

### Back

Work as for front but omit St st panel and just work the piece in garter stitch.

### Assembly

Sew back and front together. Leave top open and stuff lightly. Stitch along the narrow piece at top of purse, leaving the neck open. Sew or glue a ribbon in place at the base of the neck.

# Daisy & Honey

Knit this super cute mother and child duo to bring a smile to any little child's face. Daisy has a beautiful lacy dress with ribbon ties and Honey has her own tiny romper suit complete with a teddy motif.

· · · · · · · · · · · · · · · · · · · · · · · · · · · · · · · · · · · · · · · · · · · · · ·

## YOU WILL NEED

### For Daisy and Honey
DK/Light worsted weight (CYCA #3) yarn:
150g (approximately 510 yds) in light brown (A)
Scraps of dark brown yarn for nose and embroidered features

*Shown in:*
Sirdar Country Style DK, 40% nylon, 30% wool, 30% acrylic (170 yds/155m per 50g ball):
3 x 50g balls in 409 Naturelle

Needles size 6/4mm
Quality polyester stuffing

### For the dress and romper suit
DK/Light worsted weight (CYCA #3) yarn:
100g (approximately 358 yds) in yellow (B)
50g (approximately 179 yds) in cream (C)
Scraps of pale green (D)

*Shown in:*
Sirdar Snuggly DK, 55% nylon, 45% acrylic (179 yds/165m per 50g ball):
2 x 50g balls in 252 Lemon
1 x 50g ball in 303 Cream
Scraps in 403 Wobble

Needles size 6/4mm
2 yds/2m narrow double-sided satin baby ribbon
Bear applique motif for romper
Flower and leaf motif for dress

## KNITTING NOTES

### Gauge
22 sts and 28 rows to 4"/10cm using size 6/4mm needles.

### Yarn notes
Any DK weight yarn knitting up to a similar gauge will work for the bears.

### Measurements
Daisy is 11½"/29cm tall when sitting. Honey is 6"/15cm tall when sitting. Circumference of Daisy's belly when stuffed is about 13½"/34.5cm; Honey's belly is 7½"/19cm.

### Abbreviations
See page 33.

**Tip** The lacy pattern is a little complicated to follow, so it is best not attempted if you are a novice knitter. However, you could knit the skirt of the dress in stockinette stitch if preferred.

# Daisy
## Body and head
### made all in one piece
Using size 6/4mm needles and A, cast on 20 sts.

**Next row:** Purl.

**Next row:** Inc in each st across row (40 sts).

**Next row:** Purl.

**Next row:** *K1, inc in next st; rep from * to end of row (60 sts).

Cont even in St st until you have worked 38 more rows (mark this row for neck of bear).

Cont in St st for 24 more rows.

**Shape top of head**

**Next row:** *K4, skpo; rep from * to last st, k1 (50 sts).

**Next and following alt rows:** Purl.

**Next RS row:** *K3, skpo; rep from * to last st, k1 (40 sts).

**Next RS row:** *K2, skpo; rep from * to last st, k1 (30 sts).

**Next RS row:** *K1, skpo; rep from * to last st, k1 (20 sts).

**Next RS row:** Skpo; rep to last st, k1 (10 sts).

Purl 1 row and bind off.

## Muzzle
Using size 6/4mm needles and A, cast on 10 sts.

**Next row:** Purl.

**Next row:** Inc in each st across row (20 sts).

**Next row:** Purl.

**Next row:** *K1, inc in next st; rep from * to end of row (30 sts).

**Next row:** Purl.

**Next row:** *K2, inc in next st; rep from * to end of row (40 sts).

**Next row:** Purl.

**Next row:** *K3, inc in next st; rep from * to end of row (50 sts).

**Next row:** Purl.

**Next row:** *K4, inc in next st; rep from * to end of row (60 sts).

**Next row:** Purl.

Work 4 rows St st and bind off.

## Ears
### make 4
Using size 6/4mm needles and A,
cast on 10 sts.

**Next row:** Purl.

**Next row:** Inc in each st across
row (20 sts).

Beg with a purl row, work 9 rows
St st.

**Next row:** K2tog across row
(10 sts).

**Next row:** Purl.

**Next row:** K2tog across row and
bind off.

## Arms
### make 2
Using size 6/4mm needles and A,
cast on 10 sts.

**Next row:** Purl.

**Next row:** *K1, inc in next st; rep
from * to end of row (15 sts).

**Next row:** Purl.

**Next row:** *K1, inc in next st; rep
from * to last st, k1 (22 sts).

**Next row:** Purl.

**Next row:** Inc in first and last st
(24 sts).

Beg with a purl row, work 22 rows
in St st.

**Next row:** *K1, skpo; rep from * to
end of row (16 sts).

**Next row:** Purl.

**Next row:** K2tog across row (8 sts).

**Next row:** Purl.

**Next row:** K2tog across row (4 sts).
Break yarn and run through sts left
on needle. Draw up and fasten off.

## Legs
### make 2

Using size 6/4mm needles and A, cast on 10 sts.

**Next row:** Purl.

**Next row:** *K1, inc in next st; rep from * to end of row (15 sts).

**Next row:** Purl.

**Next row:** *K1, inc in next st; rep from * to last st, k1 (22 sts).

**Next row:** Purl.

**Next row:** Inc in first and last st (24 sts).

**Next row:** Purl.

Repeat last 2 rows once more (26 sts).

Cont in St st for 24 rows.

### Increase for foot

**Next row:** K9, inc in each of next 8 sts, k9 (34 sts).

Beg with a purl row, work 9 rows St st.

**Next row:** K2tog across row (17 sts).

**Next row:** Purl.

**Next row:** K2tog across row to last st, k1 (9 sts).

**Next row:** Purl.

Break yarn and run through sts left on needle. Draw up and fasten off.

## Nose

Using size 6/4mm needles and dark brown yarn, cast on 8 sts.

Work 4 rows St st.

**Next row:** K2tog, work to last 2 sts, k2tog (6 sts).

**Next row:** Purl.

**Next row:** K2tog, k2, k2tog (4 sts).

**Next row:** Purl.

**Next row:** K2tog twice (2 sts).

**Next row:** Purl.

**Next row:** K2tog and fasten off.

Leave a long tail of yarn to form the mouth.

# Honey
## Body and head
### made in one piece

Using size 6/4mm needles and A, cast on 10 sts.

**Next row:** Purl.

**Next row:** Inc in each st across row (20 sts).

**Next row:** Purl.

**Next row:** *K1, inc in next st; rep from * to end of row (30 sts).

**Next row:** Purl.

Work 28 rows in St st (mark this row as neckline)

Cont in St st for 14 more rows.

### Shape top of head

**Next row:** *K1, k2tog; rep from * to end of row (20 sts).

**Next row:** Purl.

**Next row:** K2tog across row (10 sts).

**Next row:** Purl.

**Next row:** K2tog across row (5 sts). Break yarn and run through sts left on needle. Draw up and fasten off.

## Arms
### make 2

Using size 6/4mm needles and A, cast on 7 sts.

**Next row:** Purl.

**Next row:** Inc in each st across row (14 sts).

**Next row:** Purl.

Work 18 rows in St st.

**Next row:** K2tog across row (7 sts).

**Next row:** Purl.

**Next row:** K2tog 3 times, k1. Break yarn and run through sts left on needle. Draw up and fasten off.

## Legs

**make 2**

Using size 6/4mm needles and A, cast on 7 sts.

**Next row:** Purl.

**Next row:** Inc in each st across row (14 sts).

**Next row:** Purl.

Work 16 rows in St st.

**Shape foot**

**Next row:** K4, inc in each of next 6 sts, k4 (20 sts).

**Next row:** Purl.

Work 4 rows in St st.

**Next row:** K2tog across row (10 sts).

**Next row:** Purl.

Repeat last 2 rows once more (5 sts).

**Next row:** K2tog twice, k1. Break yarn and run through sts left on needle. Draw up and fasten off.

## Muzzle

Using size 6/4mm needles and A, cast on 6 sts.

**Next row:** Purl.

**Next row:** Inc in each st across row (12 sts).

**Next row:** Purl.

**Next row:** *K1, inc in next st; rep from * to end of row (18 sts).

**Next row:** Purl.

**Next row:** *K2, inc in next st; rep from * to end of row (24 sts).

**Next row:** Purl.

Work 2 rows St st and bind off.

## Ears

**make 2**

Using size 6/4mm needles and A, cast on 7 sts.

Work 6 rows in St st.

**Next row:** K2tog, knit to last 2 sts, k2tog (5 sts).

**Next row:** P2tog, p1, p2tog (3 sts).

**Next row:** Inc in next st, k1, inc in last st (5 sts).

**Next row:** Inc in next st, p3, inc in last st (7 sts).

Work 6 rows in St st and bind off.

## Assembly

Begin with the head and body. Sew the seam, which runs down the back of the bear, but leave the base open to stuff. Stuff the head first, making it nice and firm and round. Thread a needle with matching yarn and, beginning at the marked row for the neck, weave the yarn in and out of each stitch all the way around, starting and ending at the seam. Pull up firmly to form the head and neck. Secure well at the seam. Continue to stuff the body, then close the base.

Sew the muzzle's side seam to form a cup shape and add some stuffing, then pin to the front of the head. Sew it in place. Pin the nose in the center of the muzzle with the widest part at the top, add a tiny bit of stuffing to pad it out slightly, then sew in place. Use the long tail of yarn left to stitch it to the base of the muzzle, pulling it firmly to form the bear's mouth.

Embroider the eyes using black yarn. Sew the ears together in pairs and attach to each side of the head.

Sew the arm seams, leaving the top open for stuffing. Attach the arms to the bear's shoulders on each side.

Sew the leg seams and stuff, making sure that you fill out the feet to a nice shape. Sew the legs to each side of the bear in a sitting position. Stitch the bow (instructions on page 131) to the top of the head.

Sew Honey together the same way except for the following differences: fold her ears with right sides together and sew the side seams. Turn right sides out, curl the ears and sew onto the head. Embroider a small nose onto the muzzle.

# Dress for Daisy
## Front

Using size 6/4mm needles and B, cast on 77 sts.

Work 3 rows in garter st.

**Row 1 (RS):** K1, *yo, sl1, k2tog, psso, yo, k5; repeat from * to last 4 sts, yo, sl1, k2tog, psso, yo, k1.

**Row 2 (and every following alt row):** Purl.

**Row 3:** Repeat row 1.

**Row 5:** K4, *yo, sl1, k1, psso, k1, k2tog, yo, k3; repeat from * to last st, k1.

**Row 7:** K1, *yo, sl1, k2tog, psso, yo, k1; rep from * to end of row.

**Row 8:** Purl.

These 8 rows form the pattern and are repeated throughout.

Work another 3 repeats of pattern.

**Next row:** (K2tog) 15 times, (k3tog) 5 times, (k2tog) 16 times (36 sts).

**Next row:** Knit.

**Next row (make eyelet holes for ribbon):** K1, *yo, k2tog; rep from * to last st, k1.

**Next row:** Knit.

Beg with a knit row, work 6 rows St st.

**Shape armholes**

Bind off 3 sts at beg of next 2 rows (30 sts).

**Next row:** K1, skpo, knit to last 3 sts, k2tog, k1 (28 sts).

**Next row:** K1, purl to last st, k1. ***
Repeat last 2 rows until 20 sts remain, ending with a purl row.

## Shape neck

**Next row:** K1, skpo, k4, turn. Leave rem sts on a stitch holder or spare needle.

**Next row:** P2tog, purl to last st, k1 (5 sts).

**Next row:** K1, skpo, k2 (4 sts).

**Next row:** P2tog, purl to end of row (3 sts).

**Next row:** Skpo, k1 (2 sts).

**Next row:** P2tog. Fasten off. Return to stitches on holder. Slip center 6 sts onto holder for center neck, rejoin yarn to rem sts and complete to match other side, working k2tog instead of skpo.

## Back

Work as front to ***

**Next row:** K1, skpo, k11, turn. Proceed on this set of sts, leaving rem sts on a holder.

**Next row:** K2, purl to last st, k1.

**Next row:** K1, skpo, knit to end.

**Next row:** K2, purl to last st, k1. Repeat last 2 rows until you have 6 sts left. Leave on a stitch holder. Rejoin yarn to remaining sts and complete to match first side, reversing shapings and working k2tog instead of skpo.

## Sleeves

### make 2

Using size 6/4mm needles and B, cast on 32 sts.

Work 3 rows in garter st.

Change to St st and work 8 rows.

#### Shape armholes

Bind off 3 sts at beg of next 2 rows (26 sts).

**Next row:** Knit.

**Next row:** K1, purl to last st, k1. Repeat last 2 rows once more.

**Next row:** K1, skpo, knit to last 3 sts, k2tog, k1 (24 sts).

**Next row:** K1, purl to last st, k1. Repeat last 2 rows until you have 10 sts.

Bind off.

## Assembly

Sew raglan seams on back, front, and sleeves. With right side of work facing and using size 6/4mm needles and B and beginning at left back, pick up and knit 6 sts from left back, 10 sts from first sleeve, 5 sts down side of neck, 6 sts from front neck, 5 sts from other side of neck, 10 sts from sleeve and finally 6 sts from right back (48 sts).

**Next row:** Knit.

**Next row (make eyelet holes for ribbon):** K1, *yo, k2tog; rep from * to last st, k1.

**Next row:** Knit.

**Next row:** Bind off.

Join side and sleeve seams. Thread ribbon through holes at neck and through holes at waist. Attach flowers and leaves to front of dress if desired using fabric glue and small stitches.

## Bow

Using size 6/4mm needles and B, cast on 8 sts.
Knit 58 rows in garter stitch.
Bind off.

## Assembly

Join the short ends. With the join at center back, fold the piece in half. Thread a needle with matching yarn and run a gathering thread through the center of the piece. Draw up firmly to shape the bow.

## Romper for Honey

### make 2

Using size 6/4mm needles and C, cast on 6 sts.
Knit 2 rows.
**Next row:** Inc 1 st at each end of row (8 sts).
**Next row:** Purl.
Repeat last 2 rows twice more (12 sts).
Cast on 2 sts at beg of the next 6 rows (24 sts).
Work 8 rows in St st.
Join in D.

Cont in St st stripe patt as follows:
Work 2 rows D, 2 rows C, 2 rows D, 2 rows C, 2 rows D. Break D.
Cont in C only, work 6 rows St st.
Change to k1, p1 rib and work 6 rows. Bind off in rib.

### Assembly

Sew in the yarn ends. With right sides together, sew the leg seams.

Now sew the side seams, matching the stripes up to the last green stripe. Overlap rib on each side for about ½"/1.5cm to form the envelope neck. Tack in place with a few stitches.

Attach the baby bear motif to front of the romper if desired using fabric glue and small stitches.

# Cute Cubs

These little bears are soft and cuddly and could be the perfect gift for a new baby. The tiny sweater with a heart motif is knitted in a simple T-shape, and the motif is added to the front of the sweater using the intarsia method for a special touch.

## YOU WILL NEED

### For each Cute Cub
DK/Light worsted weight (CYCA #3) yarn:
100g (approximately 372 yds) in pink (A)
or blue (B)
Scraps of dark gray yarn for features

*Shown in:*
Wendy Peter Pan DK, 60% acrylic, 40% nylon
(186 yds/170m per 50g ball):
2 x 50g balls in 919 Tulip or in 926 Powder Blue

Needles size 6/4mm
Needles size 3/3.25mm
Quality polyester stuffing

### For the sweaters
DK/Light worsted weight (CYCA #3) yarn:
50g (approximately 186 yds) in cream (C)

*Shown in:*
Wendy Peter Pan DK:
1 x 50g ball in 330 Soft Cream

Needles size 6/4mm

**Tip** For those who don't feel confident with intarsia, the motif can be embroidered onto the knitted fabric using the Duplicate stitch method (see page 27) or the sweaters can be left plain.

## USEFUL INFORMATION

### Gauge
24sts and 32 rows to 4"/10cm using size 6/4mm needles.

### Yarn notes
Any DK weight yarn can be substituted as long as it works up to a similar gauge. This bear is worked entirely in garter stitch.

### Measurements
8"/20cm tall when sitting. Circumference of belly when stuffed is about 11¾"/30cm.

### Abbreviations
See page 33.

# Cute Cub
### worked entirely in garter stitch
### Head

Using size 6/4mm needles and either A or B, cast on 42 sts.

Knit 4 rows.

**Next row:** K2tog at each end of row (40 sts).

Knit 2 rows.

Repeat the last 3 rows until 4 sts remain.

**Next row:** K2tog twice (2 sts).

**Next row:** K2tog and fasten off.

## Muzzle

Using either A or B and size 6/4mm needles, cast on 12 sts.

**Next row:** Knit.

**Next row:** Inc 1 st each end of row (14 sts).

Repeat last row once more (16 sts).

**Next row:** Cast on 2 sts at beg of the next 2 rows (20 sts).

Knit 6 rows.

**Next row:** Bind off 2 sts at beg of the next 2 rows (16 sts).

**Next row:** K2tog at each end of row (14 sts).

Repeat last row once more (12 sts).

Knit 2 rows.

Bind off.

## Arms

### make 2

Using size 6/4mm needles and either A or B, cast on 8 sts.

Knit 1 row.

**Next row:** Inc in each stitch across row (16 sts).

Knit 2 rows.

**Next row:** Inc 1 st at each end of next and following alt rows until you have 22 sts.

Knit 20 rows.

### Decrease for top of arm

**Next row:** K2tog at each end of row (20 sts).

**Next row:** Knit.

**Next row:** K2tog across row (10 sts).

Bind off. This is the top of the arm.

## Body

### make 2

Using either A or B and size 6/4mm needles, cast on 16 sts.

Knit 4 rows.

Inc 1 st each end of next and following alt rows until you have 26 sts.

Knit 36 rows.

Dec 1 st each end of next and following alt rows until 14 sts remain.

Bind off. This is the neck edge.

## Legs
**make 2**

Using either A or B and size 6/4mm needles, cast on 16 sts.

Knit 1 row.

**Next row:** Inc in each st across row (32 sts).

Knit 12 rows.

**Next row:** K10, k2tog 6 times, k10 (26 sts).

Knit 26 rows.

**Next row:** K2tog at each end of row (24 sts).

**Next row:** Knit.

**Next row:** K2tog across row (12 sts).

Bind off.

## Ears
**make 2**

Using either A or B and size 6/4mm needles, cast on 8 sts.

Knit 1 row.

Inc 1 st at each end of next 5 rows (18 sts).

Knit 4 rows.

**Next row:** K2tog across row (9 sts).

**Next row:** K2tog 4 times, k1 (5 sts).

Bind off.

## Assembly

Sew the head triangle together as shown in the diagram. Stuff the head firmly, shaping as you go. Pin the muzzle to the center front of the head, using the photo as a guide. Add some stuffing to pad it out and then sew it in place.

Embroider the eyes and nose with gray yarn. After working the nose, bring the yarn through the center of the nose and pull down to make a line for the mouth, pulling the yarn tight to shape of the muzzle.

Sew an ear to each corner of the head. Sew the back and front body together, leaving the neck open, and stuff firmly to a nice shape. Sew the base of the head to the body. Sew the arm and leg seams, with the seams running underneath the pieces.

Stuff each piece firmly. Sew an arm to each side of body at shoulder level. Sew the legs in place on each side of the body in a sitting positions.

FINISHING THE HEAD

# Sweater

## Back

Using size 6/4mm needles and C, cast on 33 sts.

**Row 1:** *K1, p1; rep from * to last st, k1.

Repeat last row 4 times more.

Change to St st and work 26 rows.

**Next row:** *K1, p1; rep from * to last st, k1.

Repeat last row 5 times more. Bind off.

## Front

Using size 6/4mm needles and C, cast on 33 sts.

**Row 1:** *K1, p1; rep from * to last st, k1.

Repeat last row 4 times more.

Change to St st and work 8 rows.

### Begin to work heart motif

Use 2 separate balls of C, one on each side of motif, twisting yarns together when changing colors to prevent holes in your work.

Work 13 rows from chart, reading RS rows from right to left and WS rows from left to right. The chart is worked on the center 13 stitches. First row will knit as follows:

**Row 1:** K16 C, k1 (A or B), k16 C.

After completing chart rows, cont in St st with only C, for 5 more rows.

**Next row:** *K1, p1; rep from * to last st, k1.

Repeat last row 5 times more and bind off in pattern.

## Sleeves

### make 2

Using size 6/4mm needles and C, cast on 25 sts.

**Next row:** *K1, p1; rep from * to last st, k1.

Repeat last row 4 times more.

Change to St st and work 18 rows. Bind off.

## Heart for foot

Using size 3/3.25mm needles and C, cast on 3 sts.

**Next row:** Purl.

**Next row:** Inc in each of next 2 sts, k1 (5 sts).

**Next row:** Purl.

**Next row:** Inc 1 at each end of row (7 sts).

**Next row:** Purl.

Repeat last 2 rows until you have 13 sts on the needle, ending with a purl row.

Work 2 rows in St st.

**Next row:** K2tog at each end of row (11 sts).

Divide for heart shape

**Next row:** P2tog, p3, place these 4 sts on hold; bind off 1 st, (1 st remains on rh needle) p2, p2tog.

**Next row:** K2tog twice.

**Next row:** Purl.

**Next row:** K2tog and fasten off. Return to held 4 sts and complete to match first side.

## Assembly

Sew the shoulder seams, overlapping the top at each side to form an envelope neck. Sew the sleeves to each side of back and front. Fold the sweater in half and sew the sleeve and side seams. Slip the sweater onto the bear over his legs (it's easier to put on this way.) Working from the chart, duplicate stitch a small heart in the center of the small heart made for the foot and sew it to bottom of foot.

CHART A (11 sts x 13 rows)

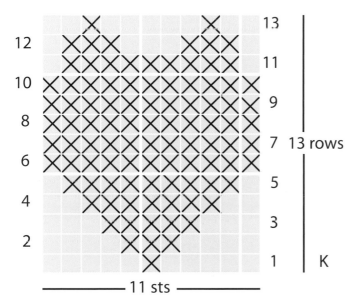

CHART B (7 sts x 6 rows)

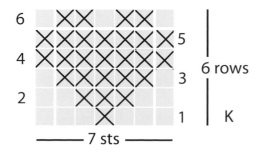

Bella

This sweet gray bear will be the perfect gift for any budding ballet dancer. With her pretty pink top, netted skirt, ribbon-tied ballet shoes, and headband with a bow, she's ready to be star of the show.

• • • • • • • • • • • • • • • • • • • • • • • • • • • • • • • • • • • • • • • • • • • • • • • • • •

## YOU WILL NEED

### For Bella
DK/Light worsted weight (CYCA #3) yarn:
200g (approximately 540 yds) in dark gray (A)
Scraps of black DK yarn for nose and features

*Shown in:*
Jarol Heritage DK, 55% wool, 25% acrylic,
20% nylon (270 yds/250m per 100g ball):
2 x 100g balls in 138 Charcoal

Needles size 6/4mm
Quality polyester stuffing

### For the ballet outfit
DK/Light worsted weight (CYCA #3) yarn:
150g (approximately 408 yds) in pink (B)

*Shown in:*
DMC Woolly DK, 100% wool (136 yds/125m
per 50g ball):
3 x 50g balls in 043 Deep Pink

Needles size 6/4mm
3¼ yds/3m of narrow satin double-sided ribbon
to match
Small piece of white net fabric approximately
16 x 8"/40 x 20cm
Fine shirring elastic
Embroidery thread in wine and medium green

## KNITTING NOTES

### Gauge
22 sts and 28 rows to 4"/10cm using size 6/4mm
needles.

### Yarn notes
Any DK weight yarn will work with this project.
Check your gauge and change needle size if
necessary.

### Measurements
10"/26cm tall when sitting. Circumference
of belly when stuffed is about 13½"/34.5cm.

### Abbreviations
See page 33.

# Bella

## Head

**Next row:** Using size 6/4mm needles and A, cast on 8 sts.

**Next row:** Purl.

**Next row:** Inc in each st across row (16 sts).

**Next row:** Purl.

**Next row:** K4, m1, k8, m1, k4 (18 sts).

**Next row:** Purl.

**Next row:** K4, m1, k1, m1, k8, m1, k1, m1, k4 (22 sts).

**Next row:** Purl.

**Next row:** K5, m1, k1, m1, k10, m1, k1, m1, k5 (26 sts).

Cont increasing in this manner until you have 66 sts, ending on a purl row.

Work 10 rows St st, decreasing 1 stitch at each end of row on the final row (64 sts).

### Decrease for back of head

**Next row:** *K6, k2tog; rep from * to end of row (56 sts).

**Next and following alt rows:** Purl.

**Next RS row:** * K5, k2tog; rep from * to end of row (48 sts).

**Next RS row:** * K4, k2tog; rep from * to end of row (40 sts).

**Next RS row:** * K3, k2tog; rep from * to end of row (32 sts).

**Next RS row:** * K2, k2tog; rep from * to end of row (24 sts).

**Next RS row:** * K1, k2tog; rep from * to end of row (16 sts).

**Next RS row:** K2tog across row (8 sts).

Break yarn and run through sts left on needle. Draw up and fasten off.

## Body

Using size 6/4mm needles and A, cast on 20 sts.

**Next row:** Purl.

**Next row:** Inc in each st across row (40 sts).

**Next row:** Purl.

**Next row:** *K1, inc in next st; rep from * to end of row (60 sts).

Cont in St st for 46 more rows.

### Decrease for top of body

**Next row:** *K4, k2tog; rep from * to end of row (50 sts).

**Next and following alt rows:** Purl.

**Next RS row:** *K3, k2tog; rep from * to end of row (40 sts).

**Next RS row:** *K2, k2tog; rep from * to end of row (30 sts).

**Next RS row:** *K1, k2tog; rep from * to end of row (20 sts).

**Next RS row:** K2tog across row (10 sts).

Break yarn and run through sts left on needle. Draw up and fasten off.

## Ears

**make 4**

Using size 6/4mm needles and A, cast on 10 sts.

Work 2 rows St st.

Inc in first and last st on every alt row to 16 sts.

Beg with a purl row, work 7 rows St st.

**Next row:** K2tog across row (8 sts).

**Next row:** Purl.

**Next row:** K2tog across row (4 sts).

Cast off

## Arms

**make 2**

Using size 6/4mm needles and A, cast on 10 sts.

**Next row:** Purl.

**Next row:** *K1, inc in next st; rep from * to end of row (15 sts).

**Next row:** Purl.

**Next row:** *K1, inc in next st; rep from * to last st, k1 (22 sts).

**Next row:** Purl.

**Next row:** Inc in first and last st (24 sts).

Beg with a purl row, work 27 rows St st.

**Next row:** *K1, skpo; rep from * to end of row (16 sts).

**Next row:** Purl.

**Next row:** K2tog across row (8 sts).

**Next row:** Purl.

**Next row:** K2tog across row (4 sts).

Break yarn and run through sts left on needle. Draw up and fasten off.

## Legs

**make 2**

Using size 6/4mm needles and A, cast on 10 sts.

**Next row:** Purl.

**Next row:** *K1, inc in next st; rep from * to end of row (15 sts).

**Next row:** Purl.

**Next row:** *K1, inc in next st; rep from * to last st, k1 (22 sts).

**Next row:** Purl.

**Next row:** Inc in first and last st (24 sts)

**Next row:** Purl.

Repeat last 2 rows once more (26 sts).

Cont in St st for 24 rows.

**Increase for foot**

**Next row:** K9, inc in each of next 8 sts, k9 (34 sts).

**Next row:** Purl.

**Next row:** K12, inc in each of next 10 sts, k12 (44 sts).

Beg with a purl row, work 9 rows St st.

**Next row:** K2tog across row (22 sts).

**Next row:** Purl.

**Next row:** K2tog across row (11 sts).

**Next row:** Purl.

**Next row:** K2tog across row to last st, k1 (6 sts).

Break yarn and run through sts left on needle. Draw up and fasten off.

Use the tail of yarn left on the nose to make the line for the mouth. Using some black yarn, embroider the eyes onto the face, and tug them a little to create indentations and add shape to the nose. Attach the head to the body. Sew the seams on the arms and legs, all seams running on the underside of the pieces. Stuff the limbs firmly and pin in position. Sew the limbs in place.

## Ballet top
### Back

Using size 6/4mm needles and B, cast on 40 sts.
Knit 3 rows.
Work 2 rows St st.
**Next row (eyelet holes):** K1, *yo, k2tog, k2; rep from * to last 3 sts, yo, k2tog, k1.
**Next row:** Purl.
Work 6 rows St st.

### Nose

Using size 6/4mm needles and black yarn, cast on 8 sts.
Work 4 rows in St st.
**Next row:** K2tog, work to last 2 sts, K2tog (6 sts).
**Next row:** Purl.
**Next row:** K2tog, k2, k2tog (4 sts).
**Next row:** Purl.
**Next row:** K2tog twice.
**Next row:** Purl.
**Next row:** K2tog and fasten off. Leave a long tail of yarn to form the mouth.

### Assembly

Sew the body seam, which runs down the back, and stuff firmly before closing. Sew the head seam and stuff firmly, as for the body. Sew the ears together in pairs, curling them inward as you sew. Sew the ears to each side of the head. Pin the nose in place on the head and pad it out with a little stuffing before stitching it in place.

**Begin armhole shaping**

Bind off 4 sts at the beg of the next 2 rows (32 sts).

**Next row:** K2, skpo, knit to last 4 sts, k2tog, k2 (30 sts).

**Next row:** K2, purl to last 2 sts, k2.

Repeat last 2 rows until you have 12 sts.

Bind off.

## Sleeves

### make 2

Follow instructions as for back but work 4 rows St st instead of 6.

## Left front

Using size 6/4mm needles and B, cast on 40 sts.

Knit 3 rows.

**Next row:** Knit.

**Next row:** K2, purl to end.

**Next row (eyelet holes):** K1, *yo, k2tog, k2; rep from * to last 7 sts, yo, k2tog, k5.

**Next row:** K2, purl to end of row.

**Next row:** Knit to last 4 sts, k2tog, k2 (39 sts).

**Next row:** K2, purl to end of row.

Repeat last 2 rows twice more.

## Begin armhole shaping

Bind off 4sts, knit to last 4 sts, k2tog, k2 (32 sts).

**Next row:** K2, purl to last 2 sts, k2.

**Next row:** K2, skpo, knit to last 4 sts, k2tog, k2 (30 sts).

**Next row:** K2, p2tog, purl to last 2 sts, k2 (29 sts).

**Next row:** Dec at armhole edge on every alt row and *at the same time* dec on front edge on every row until you have 5 sts.

Knit 4 rows garter stitch and bind off.

## Right front

Using size 6/4mm needles and B, cast on 40 sts.

Knit 3 rows.

**Next row:** Knit.

**Next row:** Purl to last 2 sts, k2.

**Next row (eyelet holes):** K5, *yo, k2tog, k2; rep from * to last 3 sts, yo, k2tog, k1.

**Next row:** Purl to last 2 sts, k2.

**Next row:** K2, skpo, knit to end (39 sts).

**Next row:** Purl to last 2 sts, k2.

Repeat last 2 rows twice more.

**Next row:** K2, skpo, knit to end (36 sts).

## Begin armhole shaping

**Next row:** Bind off 4 sts, purl to last 2 sts, k2 (32 sts).

**Next row:** K2, skpo, knit to end (31 sts).

**Next row:** K2, p2tog, purl to last 4 sts, p2tog tbl, k2 (29 sts).

**Next row:** K2, skpo, knit to end (28 sts).

**Next row:** Dec at armhole edge on every alt row and *at the same time* dec at front edge on every row to 5 sts.

Knit 4 rows garter stitch and bind off.

## Assembly

Join the sleeve seams neatly to the back and fronts. Join the sleeve and side seams. Cut the ribbon to the appropriate length and thread through the holes at the base of the top. Sew two shorter pieces of ribbon at each side seam to tie the top. Thread ribbon through the sleeves and neatly sew the ends together on the inside of the sleeve. Using the wine and green embroidery thread, embroider flowers and leaves onto one side of the top if desired.

## Skirt

### make 2

Using size 6/4mm needles and B, cast on 42 sts.

Knit 2 rows.

**Next row:** K13, m1, p1, m1, k14, m1, p1, m1, k13 (46 sts).

**Next row:** P13, k3, p14, k3, p13.

**Next row:** K13, m1, p3, m1, k14, m1, p3, m1, k13 (50 sts).

**Next row:** P13, k5, p14, k5, p13.

**Next row:** K13, m1, p5, m1, k14, m1, p5, m1, k13 (54 sts).

**Next row:** P13, k7, p14, k7, p13.

Continue to increase in this manner, adding 1 st each side of the panels on every alt row, until you have 15 sts in each panel.

**Next row:** K13, p15, k14, p15, k13.

**Next row:** P13, k15, p14, k15, p13.

Repeat last 2 rows 3 times more. Work 4 rows garter stitch and bind off.

## Assembly

Before sewing the seam of the skirt, measure its length and depth. Using the skirt as a template, cut a piece of net twice as long and twice as deep as the skirt. Fold the net in half lengthways; the folded end will be at the bottom of the skirt. Pin the top edge closed. Thread a needle with some shirring elastic and sew a neat running stitch all along the edge, sewing through both thicknesses of net. Gather up to fit the waist of the skirt. Stitch neatly to the inside of waist of the skirt. Sew the back seam neatly. Join the side seams.

Thread shirring elastic through the top of the skirt, weaving in and out of the fabric. Tie the elastic in a tight knot, and work in the ends.

## Headband

Using size 6/4mm needles and B,
cast on 76 sts.
Knit 4 rows and bind off.

### Bow

Using size 6/4mm needles and B,
cast on 7 sts.
Knit 60 rows.
Bind off.

### Assembly

Sew the short ends of the headband
together, then sew the short ends
of the bow together. Fold in half
with the seam at the center back.

Run a gathering thread through
the center of the piece and draw
up to form a bow shape. Sew the
bow to the center of the headband.
Embroider flowers and leaves into
the center of the bow if desired.

## Shoes

**make 2**

Using size 6/4mm needles and B,
cast on 8 sts.
**Next row:** Purl.
**Next row:** Inc in each st across
row (16 sts).
**Next row:** Purl.
**Next row:** *K1, inc in next st; rep
from * to end of row (24 sts).
**Next row:** Purl.
**Next row:** *K2, inc in next st; rep
from * to end of row (32 sts).
**Next row:** Purl.

**Next row:** *K3, inc in next st; rep
from * to end of row (40 sts).
Work in St st for 10 rows.
**Next row:** K1, *yo, k2tog, k2;
rep from * to last 3 sts, yo,
k2tog, k1.
**Next row:** Purl.
Knit 2 rows and cast off.

### Assembly

Sew the back seam. Thread ribbon
through the holes at the ankles.

Benji

Everyone will love this skateboarder bear with his endearing face and his own special hoodie complete with ears! He even has his own skateboard, making him the coolest bear around. He is made in a soft brushed yarn and is just waiting to be hugged.

•••••••••••••••••••••••••••••••••••••••••••••••••••••••••••

## YOU WILL NEED

### For Benji
Bulky weight (CYCA #6) yarn:
100g (approximately 240 yds) in light gray (A)
Scraps of black DK yarn for nose (B)

*Shown in:*
Sirdar Freya, 55% cotton, 31% acrylic, 14% polyester (120 yds/110m per 50g ball):
2 x 50g balls in 857 Gosling

Needles size 9/5.5mm
Needles size 6/4mm
Quality polyester stuffing
1 pair of black button safety eyes

### For the hoodie
DK/Light worsted weight (CYCA #3) yarn:
50g (approximately 170 yds) in green (C)
50g (approximately 170 yds) in yellow (D)

*Shown in:*
Sirdar Country Style DK, 40% nylon, 30% wool, 30% acrylic (170 yds/155m per 50g ball):
1 x 50g ball in 614 Meadow
1 x 50g ball in 399 Honey

Needles size 6/4mm

### For the skateboard
DK/Light worsted weight (CYCA #3) yarn
50g (approximately 164 yds) in gray (E)
50g (approximately 170 yds) in yellow (F)

50g (approximately 164 yds) in lime green
Scraps of blue (G)

*Shown in:*
Sirdar Country Style DK:
1 x 50g ball in 399 Honey
Robin DK, 100% acrylic (82 yds/75m per 25g ball)
2 x 25g ball 6392 Seal
2 x 25g ball in 162 Cordial

Needles size 6/4mm
Stiff cardstock
Craft glue

## KNITTING NOTES

### Gauge
15 sts and 20 rows to 4"/10cm in St st for bulky yarn using size 9/5.5mm needles.
22 sts and 28 rows to 4"/10cm in St st for DK yarn using size 6/4mm needles.

### Yarn notes
Any tweedy-type yarn with a gauge to match the bear will do if you need to substitute yarns.

### Measurements
11"/28cm tall when sitting. Circumference of belly when stuffed is about 14"/35.5cm.

### Abbreviations
See page 33.

# Benji

## Head

Using size 9/5.5mm needles and A, cast on 10 sts.

**Next row:** Purl.

**Next row:** Inc in each st across row (20 sts).

Beg with a purl row, work 3 rows St st.

**Next row:** *K1, inc in next st; repeat from * to end of row (30 sts).

Beg with a purl row, work 3 rows St st.

**Next row:** *K1, inc in next st; repeat from * to end of row (45 sts).

Beg with a purl row, work 11 rows St st.

### Shape top of head

**Next row:** *K1, k2tog; rep from * to end of row (30 sts).

Beg with a purl row, work 3 rows st st.

**Next row:** K2tog across row (15 sts).

**Next row:** Purl.

Break yarn and run through sts left on needle. Draw up and fasten off.

## Muzzle

Using size 9/5.5mm needles and A, cast on 8 sts.

**Next row:** Purl.

**Next row:** Inc in each stitch across row (16 sts).

**Next row:** Purl.

**Next row:** *K1, inc in next st; rep from * to end of row (24 sts).

**Next row:** Purl.

**Next row:** *K2, inc in next st; rep from * to end of row (32 sts).

Beg with a purl row, work 7 rows St st.

Bind off.

## Nose

Using size 6/4mm needles and B, cast on 8 sts.

Work 6 rows garter st.

Dec 1 st at each end of next and following alt rows to 2 sts.

**Next row:** K2tog, fasten off, leaving a long tail of yarn.

## Body

Using size 9/5.5mm needles and A, cast on 10 sts.

**Next row:** Purl.

**Next row:** Inc in each st across row (20 sts).

Beg with a purl row, work 3 rows st st.

**Next row:** *K1, inc in next st; rep from * to end of row (30 sts).

Beg with a purl row, work 3 rows st st.

**Next row:** *K1, inc in next st; rep from * to end of row (45 sts).

Beg with a purl row, work 31 rows St st.

### Shape top of body

**Next row:** *K1, k2tog; rep from * to end of row (30 sts).

Beg with a purl row, work 3 rows St st.

**Next row:** K2tog across row (15 sts).

**Next row:** Purl.

Break yarn and run through sts left on needle. Draw up and fasten off.

## Legs

make 2

Using size 9/5.5mm needles and A, cast on 8 sts.

**Next row:** Purl.

**Next row:** Inc in each st across row (16 sts).

Work in St st for 5 rows.

**Next row:** Inc 1 st at each end of row (18 sts).

Work 3 rows St st.

**Next row:** *K2, inc in next st; rep from * to end of row (24 sts).

Work 17 rows St st.

**Next row:** K8, inc in each of next 8 sts, k8 (32 sts).
**Next row:** Purl.
Work 8 rows st st.
**Next row:** K2tog across row (16 sts).
**Next row:** Purl.
Repeat last 2 rows once more. Break yarn and run through sts left on needle. Draw up and fasten off.

## Arms
### make 2
Using size 9/5.5mm needles and A, cast on 8 sts.
**Next row:** Purl.
**Next row:** Inc in each st across row (16 sts).
**Next row:** Purl.
**Next row:** Inc 1 st at each end of row (18 sts).
**Next row:** Purl.
**Next row:** Inc 1 st at each end of row (20 sts).

**Next row:** Purl.
Work 18 rows St st.
**Next row:** K2tog across row (10 sts).
**Next row:** Purl.
**Next row:** K2tog across row (5 sts).
**Next row:** Purl.
Break yarn and run through sts left on needle. Draw up and fasten off.

## Ears
### make 2
Using size 9/5.5mm needles and A, cast on 10 sts.
**Next row:** Purl.
**Next row:** Inc in each st across row (20 sts).
Work 5 rows St st.
**Next row:** K2tog across row (10 sts).
**Next row:** Purl.
**Next row:** K2tog across row (5 sts).
Bind off.

## Assembly
Sewing with this type of yarn is challenging. Use a big-eyed, blunt-ended needle and short lengths of yarn. Seams will run down the back of the head and body, and the undersides of the arms and legs.

Sew the body seam first, leaving the cast-on end open to stuff. Stuff firmly to a nice rounded shape. Close the opening.

Sew the head and sew the same way as the body, leaving an opening to stuff. Stuff firmly.

Sew the arm seams, leaving the cast-on edge open for stuffing. To stuff the arms, push plenty of stuffing down into the paw first, then continue stuffing the rest of the arm.

Sew the leg seams, leaving the top open to stuff. Stuff firmly, pushing extra stuffing into the feet.

## Assembly, cont'd

Sew the muzzle seam, which runs underneath. Pin to the front of the bear's head and add stuffing. It will take a bit patience to get it to look right. Sew the muzzle onto the face, adding more stuffing for a good shape. Sew the nose onto the center of the muzzle.

Insert safety eyes on each side of the head, just above the muzzle. Click into place and close the base of the head.

Pin the ears onto the head on each side, making them level. With some matching yarn, curl the ears into a semicircular shape, then stitch them in place.

Pin the legs to the body in a sitting position, making them level. Sew the legs in place. Pin the arms in position and sew firmly in place. Finally, sew the bear's head onto the body.

# Hoodie
## Back

Using size 6/4mm needles and C, cast on 38 sts.

Work in double seed st as follows:

**Row 1:** *K2, p2; repeat from * to last 2 sts, k2.

**Row 2:** *P2, k2; repeat from * to last 2 sts, p2.

**Row 3:** *P2, k2; repeat from * to last 2 sts, p2.

**Row 4:** *K2, p2; repeat from * to last 2 sts, k2.

Repeat first 2 rows once more.

Change to St st and work 16 rows.

**Shape arms**

Bind off 2 sts at beg of next 2 rows (34 sts).

**Next row:** K1, skpo, knit to last 3 sts, k2tog, k1 (32 sts).

**Next row:** K1, purl to last st, k1.

Repeat last 2 rows to 14 sts, ending with a purl row.

Bind off.

## Sleeves
### make 2

Using size 6/4mm needles and C, cast on 36 sts.

Work 4 rows in double seed st.

Join in D, change to St st and work in stripes of 2 rows D, 2 rows C, for 14 rows.

**Keeping in stripe pattern as set, shape armholes**

Bind off 2 sts at beg of next 2 rows (32 sts).

Work 2 rows in St st.

**Next row:** K1, skpo, knit to last 3 sts, k2tog, k1 (30 sts).

**Next row:** K1, purl to last st, k1.

Repeat last 2 rows to 12 sts, ending with a purl row.

Bind off.

## Right front

Using size 6/4mm needles and C, cast on 20 sts.

Work in double seed st as follows:

**Row 1:** *K2, p2; repeat from * to end of row.

**Row 2:** *P2, k2; repeat from * to end of row.

**Row 3:** *P2, k2; repeat from * to end of row.

**Row 4:** *K2, p2; repeat from * to end of row.

Repeat first 2 rows once more.

Change to St st with double seed st front border.

**Next row:** P2, k2, p2, knit to end of row.

**Next row:** Purl to last 6 sts, k2, p2, k2.

Keeping double seed st border as established, work 13 more rows. (Work 14 rows for left front.)

**Shape armhole**

**Next row:** Bind off 2 sts, work in pattern to end of row (18 sts).

**Next row:** Work in pattern to last 3 sts, k2tog, k1 (17 sts)

**Next row:** K1, work in pattern to end of row.

Repeat last 2 rows twice more (15 sts).

**Shape neck**

**Next row:** Bind off 6 sts, work in pattern to last 3 sts, k2tog, k1 (8 sts).

**Next row:** K1, purl to end of row.

Cont to dec at armhole edge in this manner until 2 sts remain, k2tog and fasten off.

## Left front

Work as for right front but reverse border and shapings.

## Hood

Begin at back.

Using size 6/4mm needles and C, cast on 24 sts.

Work in striped pattern as for sleeves for 28 rows.

**Next 2 rows:** Keeping striped pattern as set, cast on 24 sts, work to end (72 sts).

Cont in stripes for 16 more rows.

Work 4 rows double seed st in C only. Bind off.

## Ears

**make 2**

Using size 6/4mm needles and D, cast on 6 sts.

Work 2 rows St st.

Inc 1 st at each end of next and alt rows to 10 sts.

Work 16 rows St st.

Dec 1 st at each end of next and following alt rows to 6 sts.

Work 2 rows St st and bind off.

## Assembly

Sew the sleeves to back and fronts. Using size 6/4mm needles and C, join yarn to right front neck edge after bound off stitches, then pick up and knit 6 sts along neck edge, 12 sts from first sleeve, 14 sts across back, 12 sts from second sleeve, and 6 sts down left front neck edge (50 sts).

**Next row:** *K2, p2; rep from * to last 2 sts, k2.

**Next row:** *P2,k; rep from * to last 2 sts, P2.

Bind off firmly.

Sew in the yarn ends, join the side and sleeve seams. Join the short sides of the hood to the back to form the hood. Pin the base of the hood all around the neck band, easing if necessary. Sew neatly in place. Fold the ear in half, join short sides, and turn right-side out. Sew the base of the ear to corner of hood. Repeat with second ear. Make two twisted cords in D, join to each side of the fronts, and tie into a bow.

# Skateboard
## Back and front
**make 1 in E and 1 in F for both back and front, 4 pieces total**

Using size 6/4mm needles and appropriate color, cast on 14 sts.
Work 2 rows in St st.
**Next row:** Inc in first and last st (16 sts).
**Next row:** Purl.
Cast on 2 sts at the beg of the next 4 rows (24 sts).
Work 14 rows St st.
**Next row:** K2tog at each end of row (22 sts).
**Next row:** Purl.
Work 20 rows St st.
Bind off 2 sts at the beg of the next 6 rows (10 sts).
Bind off remaining 10 sts.

## Wheels
### make 4

Using size 6/4mm needles and G, cast on 10 sts.
Knit 34 rows garter st and bind off.

## Axles
### make 2

Using size 6/4mm needles and E, cast on 36 sts.
Work 14 rows in St st and bind off.

## Wheel inners
### make 4

Using size 6/4mm needles and blue yarn, cast on 3 sts.
**Next row:** Knit.
**Next row:** K1, inc in next st, k1 (4 sts).
**Next row:** Knit.
**Next row:** Knit.
**Next row:** K1, k2tog, k1 (3 sts).
**Next row:** K3tog and fasten off.

## Assembly

Cut a piece of cardstock into an oblong 7½"/19cm x 4¼"/11cm. Round off the top and bottom, tapering the top third of the board slightly. With right sides facing, sew the two pieces of the board together, leaving the base open. Turn right sides out. Carefully spread a little craft glue all around the top edge of the cardstock. Slip it carefully into the knitted piece and press down firmly all around the edges. Sew the base neatly closed.

Roll a tube of cardstock into a cylinder measuring 6½"/16cm long and 2½"/7cm in circumference. Glue the edges together firmly. Sew the long edges of the axle covering together to form a tube. Push the cardstock tube inside.

Fold a wheel piece in half lengthwise and join the short ends to form a ring. Do the same with the other three wheels. Slip a wheel onto both ends of the axles and glue them in place. You may also sew in place to make them extra secure. Sew or glue the wheel inners in place inside each wheel. Pin axles to base of skateboard and glue or sew in place.

## Suppliers

Below is a list of suppliers' websites and links for the yarns and materials used in this book. Some suppliers will stock all of the yarns required and many ship worldwide. Although specific yarns are listed in each pattern, most yarns can be substituted as long as they have a similar tension.

### FOR THE USA

**Hobby Lobby**
www.hobbylobby.com

**Jo-Ann fabric and craft stores**
www.joann.com

**Michael's Stores**
www.michael's.com

**Target**
www.Target.com

**Wal-Mart**
www.walmart.com

Find your local yarn shop:
www.knitmap.com
www.yarngroup.org
www.yarnshop.sweaterbabe.com

If you are substituting brands of yarn, be sure to do a gauge swatch. Yarn companies Bernat, Caron, Lion Brand Yarn, Patons, and Red Heart all offer helpful information on yarn substitution.
**Bernat** www.bernat.com
**Caron** www.caron.com
**Lion Brand** Yarn www.lionbrand.com
**Red Heart** www.redheart.**com**

### OTHER YARN SOURCES

**Begère de France**
www.bergeredefrance.co.uk
*For contacts in Europe and worldwide:*
www.bergeredefrance.com

**Hobbycraft**
Hobbycraft stores are located all over the UK. They stock just about everything you will need to create the bears, from yarns and needles, to toy stuffing and fabric glues:
www.hobbycraft.co.uk

**Rico Yarns**
Rico Design GmbH & Co. KG
Industriestr. 19–23
33034 Brakel
Germany
+49 (0) 52 72 602-0
info@rico-design.de

**Sirdar Yarns**
Flanshaw Lane
Wakefield
West Yorkshire,
WF2 9ND
UK
+44 (0)1924 231682
www.sirdar.co.uk/storelocator
www.sirdar.co.uk/contactus/
findsirdarworldwide

**Wendy Wools Ltd**
Thomas B. Ramsden
Gordon Mills
Netherfield Road
Guiseley
West Yorkshire,
LS20 9PD
UK
+44 (0)1943 872 264
www.tbramsden.co.uk

## About the author

Val's passion for knitting and needlecrafts began when she was a little girl: her father taught her to knit when she was just five years old. As she grew up she became more proficient at knitting and began to work for spinners and designers, checking knitting patterns and making garments for photography. She decided to make her own creations and soon knitting magazines were publishing her work on a regular basis. About five years ago she wrote her first book, which became very popular, and she went on to write many more bestselling knitting and crochet books, which are available worldwide. Val also teaches knitting and crochet, and lives and works in Shropshire in the UK. Her website can be found at www.crossedneedles.co.uk

## Acknowledgments

Many thanks to Sirdar, Rico, Bergère de France and Thomas Ramsden for their kind supply of some of the yarns used in the books. A big thank you to Dominique Page and everyone at GMC for their never-ending help, encouragement and wonderful work in producing this gorgeous publication. And last but not least, thank you to all my family and friends who have supported me and offered endless advice and help while I was creating all the bears in the book.

## Index

To place an order, or to request a catalog, contact

**The Taunton Press, Inc.**
63 South Main Street, P.O. Box 5506
Newtown, CT 06470-5506
Tel: (800) 888-8286
www.taunton.com